The Messiah People
Jim Punton

Punton Papers
Volume 1

Edited by Paul Grant and Raj Patel

September 1993
A Hot Iron Press Publication, Carrs Lane Church Centre,
Carrs Lane, Birmingham B4 7SX

The editors would like to thank Jeanne, Andrew, Carla, Maurice, Michael and Surjit for their invaluable help in realising this project.

The Messiah People was first published by the Hot Iron Press, the Black and Third World Theology Group, Carrs Lane Church Centre, Carrs Lane, Birmingham B4 7SX

Photo courtesy of Scripture Union
Printed by the Russell Press, Nottingham

ISBN 0 9519492 2 5 The Messiah People (pbk)

CONTENTS

Introduction

It was in 1978 that Jim paid his first visit to Post Green. The circumstances that led to his coming are interesting.

The previous year Jim had been in Australia, visiting and speaking to Christian groups and communities. He shared with them his vision of the Messiah community. Almost immediately on his heels followed Graham Pulkingham (at that time Provost of the Cathedral of the Isles in Cumbrae). Graham too had a story to tell about community, in particular the way in which his own community - the Community of the Celebration - had grown out of an outreach programme of the parish community of the Church of the Redeemer, Houston, Texas, USA.

Graham had become a close friend to those of us at Post Green, and in a conversation following his visit to Australia, Graham said to me, 'Two people you should think of being in touch with, Jeanne, are Bishop Colin Winter (then Bishop of Namibia-in-exile), and a man called Jim Punton. I don't know much about him, but wherever I went in Australia people told me, "What you are telling us is exactly the same message that Jim Punton brought to us. The one difference is that you are sharing about that message being lived out in practice in an actual community committed to the same values and ideals."'

When Graham said this, I laughed. 'Well, it won't be difficult for me to invite Jim Punton down here. I already know him, and indeed he lives in the flat I vacated in Streatham five years ago.' (My life story has its own close connections with Frontier Youth Trust, and from 1961 to 1968 I lived and worked in Streatham as the youth Leader attached to Immanuel Church - Immanuel Youth Club being part of the Knights' Association of Christian Youth Clubs.)

So Jim was invited and duly came. His impact upon us all was so immediate and intense that before he left to return to London we had invited him back to speak at one of our camps that summer. Our impact upon Jim must have been considerable too since his answer was to say that if there was any anyway in which he could arrange it at such short notice, he would. And he did, and kept coming back.

This is the background to the edited transcripts that form this book. The talks on the Messianic Vision, Fellowship, Task and Mind were delivered at that first summer camp. The two studies on Luke, presented here as Announcing the Messiah and the Messianic Jubilee, were given to the community at a later date, but have been included to further flesh out Jim's thinking on the Messiah.

Jim's death in 1986 was a hard blow to me, and to the Community, as to so many of this friends in these isles and throughout the world. In the intervening years from 1978 he almost became a part of the Community. Indeed, we were told that on his travels Jim spoke as though he was a member of the Community, so closely did he identify himself with it.

When he came to stay, he taught us, drawing on his years of studying the biblical texts, interpreting to us something about the life we were seeking to live and deepening and broadening our understanding of its significance for us and for what he saw the Spirit of God doing in the intentional communities of that period, of which we were but one. At the same time, he was always a warm and perceptive pastor to many within the community, and to all of us a close and dear friend. His teachings to us or to the camps at which he spoke were an extraordinary potent mixture of Jim's deep love of the word and lifelong study of the biblical texts, and of his own passionate involvement in living a 'kingdom centred life'. Also of his obvious love for and deep concern for one 'Messiah community', struggling with all the longings and ambiguities of how to live shalom in the realities our own human weaknesses and the complexities of living such a life in the nineteen seventies and eighties.

One small story tells this tale. In the teachings on Luke Jim tells of how one day a member of one of our Cottage Farm household (where Jim usually stayed) was given a gift of a pair of shoes. We were always excited when such gifts arrived because they were always very timely and certainly much needed. Those were the days when we had a common purse which enabled us to live simply although not uncomfortably, and personal spending money was limited to 50p a week. Essential clothing was provided through our household allowances, and forays in our community 'swap shop', to which many good friends contributed clothing - and often through unexpected and timely gifts. For us a gift of a pair of shoes was an occasion for 'hoorays', laughter and relief that one such need had been met. For Jim, as he was to tell the tale often, it was a moment when he could hardly keep back the tears.

We did not retain the common purse at Post Green beyond 1987. The community has its own story of dying, grieving and also of rising again slowly and with difficulty to fragile growth and a renewed vision of its future. Jim saw the beginning of this period in our life, but by that time was not well himself.

Jim and I had often talked of the possibility that a small group of the Community might relocate to an inner-city area, and there form a community around the concerns of GrassRoots magazine (a kind of mini-Sojourners). That almost took place, but circumstances intervened. Jim might have moved to join that household. A lot of hopes died the year that Jim died, although I can see in retrospect the Spirit was already seeding new possibilities. It was not however easy to see it that way at that time.

Jim died in May 1986. For three years previously a small group of us (Jim included), had been meeting to plan a visit from Jim Wallis (editor of Sojourners magazine) - a preaching tour of England, Scotland and Wales. The two Jims were friends, and the Sojourners Community already had close links with Post Green and with the Communities of Celebration in Scotland and in the USA. Jim Wallis had asked that Jim Punton and I travel with him, and we had agreed to do so.

Jim Punton's Memorial Service in South London took place during the tour and I wondered that I could have been so stupid as to agree to say anything. Wandering around the park by Llandaff Cathedral in Wales (on our Cardiff stop) I tried to think of something to say. Now I can recall little of what I thought then or later said at the Memorial Service, except that it concerned Jim's gut sense that we Christians were being 'messiahed' for the God-given task of birthing the good news of Jesus in a difficult period of our history. 'Difficult, and it's going to get worse,' he once said to me. I remembered that as I walked that day and thought about all those we had met on the tour whose hunger for the message Jim Wallis brought was obvious, and also obvious was their need of supportive places - little communities - that could help and encourage them to be the church - a new way of being church.

Jim Wallis said often on the tour that he felt that Jim was with us. Mostly I did not or could not feel it at that time, but there have been times since when I have felt that closeness. I felt this again recently as I listened to the Luke and Messiah teachings on tape. I had agreed to write this introduction, and then realised that I was going to have difficulty recalling their context unless I listened to Jim himself... on tape.

What is written in this book does recapture much of the quality of Jim's teaching, but hearing Jim on tape is even better. There are comments and interaction too with members of the community. It brought it all back, and I found to my great relief that I was laughing and loving it. But even more profoundly I realised these were words spoken, yes, to one community at a moment in its history, but more than that the words for this moment too. A prophetic word for us all that here as we continue to we to live shalom through the nineties and into the twenty-first century.

All this encourages and excites me, and also challenges. It is impossible to listen to Jim and not be challenged. Yet always his challenging us comes as it came with a deep compassionate understanding that to live such a 'discipled life' is not easy, and indeed impossible unless lived as part of a community of discipleship. And that only with the help of God of Spirit who messiahs us individually and together.

There has been a sense of 'God's clock' in the thinking that has gone into the production of this book. After Jim had died a few of us worked on collecting together his papers and the tapes made of his teachings at Post Green, Greenbelt and elsewhere. The idea was to bring out some kind of publication. Marshall Pickering funded the project, Val Nobbs (who had worked on GrassRoots magazine) collected the materials and the London Mennonite Centre gave them a home. Later Alison Lyon (also one of the team who travelled with Jim Wallis in 1986) transcribed the Luke and the Messiah teachings. I was then to work on the text. But by that time Marshall Pickering had been taken over by another publishing house, the Editors interested in the project had moved, and there was no longer funding or an interested publisher. And I failed in my task!

I think perhaps then was not the right time. Now feels more like it. And I am glad that this book is being produced in Post Green's 25th anniversary year. It captures for us at Post Green and for our friends something of the essence of what was happening among us at that time. Some of the interaction between Jim and the community has been taken out in the editing of the material for this booklet, but is still there on the tapes. During the period that Jim was visiting us regularly, we also had considerable input from Andrew Kirk as our theological consultant, and from Alan and Eleanor Krieder. The community would not be where it is today but for their input. Much has changed in the years since, but the orientation of the community - a kind of kingdom orientation - has not changed, but rather deepened. For those who would like to know more of what has happened to the community in the years since, there are other publications available.

I have been listening to Jim's tapes and thinking about this written introduction during Lent 1993. Again and again I have been struck by the sense of our one-ness with the 'living dead' as we continue on the Messiah Way. That brings Jim close, as so many others. This is a time when there is a resurgence of interest in Celtic spirituality - so important for those of us who live in these islands. And it is here in these Celtic writings that I find the words that express what I feel about this -

'the thread of life that binds the living and the dead.'

Jeanne Hinton
May 1993

Jeanne Hinton is the author of *'Communities: the stories and spirituality of twelve European communities'*, published by Eagle.

The Messianic Vision

The Spirit of the Lord

Well, I'm really thrilled to be here. Paul stood several times before people, as he said, 'with apprehensions' - and I do have apprehensions, but part of my apprehension is that I'm always scared of things that God wants to do because of what it calls from us. And I know that there's not one of us going to leave this time together the same person that we came. We're going to be challenged by God, unquestionably, in our togetherness, by His Spirit to a new obedience. And we're either going to say "Yes, God, by your grace I will move into that new obedience", or we're going to falter and we're going to move further back in our discipleship.

And I believe that we've got a tremendous and terrific and beautiful opportunity to discover, in our togetherness over these next few days, what it is to be God's people in a broken world and to take from this place new love, new understanding, new freedom, new openness to God's Spirit, new awareness of what it is to belong. And along with that sense of belonging, a new commitment to the little people, to the needy, to the oppressed, to the hurt, to those in need of healing.

You know, if God could hold in His hands a group this size of young men and women committed to Jesus Christ, He could do something very beautiful and very remarkable. And I believe, I know, He wants to do that remarkable thing. So I don't apologise that we're going to be looking quite seriously at the nature of the Gospel today. I believe even those of us who have a very profound experience of God's Spirit may yet be missing out on an understanding of what the gospel really is and what God is calling us to.

I've been invited to introduce, to open up, God's word on the area of what it means to be the Messiah People. Tonight we're going to look at the vision - the Messianic Vision - that is held before us in God's word.

And I'm going to read (if you're accustomed to always reading, perhaps you might want to listen; if you're someone who always listens, it might be good to turn up the book) Luke, chapter four. I'm reading verses, 1 and 2, 14-19, then 43, so if I'm jumping you're going to have to jump with me!

'And Jesus, full of the Holy Spirit, returned from the Jordan and was led by the Spirit for forty days in the wilderness, tempted by the devil... And Jesus returned, in the power of the Spirit into Galilee. And a report concerning Him went out through all the surrounding country and He taught in their synagogues, being glorified by all.

'And He came to Nazareth, where He had been brought up and He went to the synagogue as His custom was on the Sabbath day. And He stood up to read and there was given to Him the scroll of the prophet Isaiah. He opened the book and found the place where it was written: "The Spirit of the Lord is upon me because He has anointed me to preach good news to the poor, He has sent me to proclaim deliverance to the captives and recovering of sight to the blind, to set at liberty those who are oppressed, to proclaim the acceptable year of the Lord."'

And later in verse 43: Jesus said to the people, 'I must proclaim the good news of the kingdom of God to other cities also, for I was sent for this purpose.'

The Good News of Jesus

I wonder if you notice (apart from the place of the Holy Spirit in all of that story, to which we must return), what the good news of the gospel was for Jesus. Many of us here, rejoicing in the fact that God, in His love, has laid His hand upon us and has given us the experience of new life through Jesus Christ, believe that the good news is about personal conversion, that the good news is about rebirth. But I want to suggest to you that the good news we find Jesus proclaiming is good news of the kingdom of God, good news of God's reign; that Jesus is, in fact, talking about and announcing and bringing, in Himself, a new order; that the good news is of the new order of existence that Jesus has come to bring, to demonstrate, to make possible. And the gateway into the new kingdom is by the new birth.

But the good news is of what lies beyond the new birth. The good news is good news of the reign of God. The good news of God's kingdom - a whole new order, a whole new humanity, a whole new creation. And so long as we stop at proclaiming good news which takes people just across the threshold, we are stopping short of a proclamation of the good news that Jesus was proclaiming and embodying. Jesus came that there might be a new humanity. And the disciple group around Him were the beginnings of God's new humanity, giving expression in their relationships, in their togetherness, in their new peoplehood, to the kingdom or reign of God.

We've not got a great deal of time, but I would like to give us a little of the background as we have it in the Old Testament because this concept of God's reign, or God's kingdom to be experienced now, goes right back into the Old Testament. The content of God's reign is caught up in several themes. And some of you who know me quite well know that one of these has revolutionised my own understanding of the gospel and shown me a great deal of beauty in my understanding of God's truth: the Hebrew word shalom.

The reign of shalom

Again and again in the Hebrew scriptures the content of the kingdom of God, the content of God's reign is described as shalom. Now we have rendered this - I don't know what it is in Swedish, perhaps you get closer to it there, but we have rendered it in English by the word peace. Unfortunately, the word peace simply gets nowhere near the richness of the Hebrew word shalom. It is a word which comes from a verb meaning to make complete, to bring into completeness, to bring into wholeness and it refers to the totality of well-being when a thing is whole as it was intended to be. For the individual person, that person was experiencing God's shalom (let's notice that it's God's shalom - shalom is always a gift of God and not something which people create - shalom is God's gift) when his or her person is in wholeness.

Wholeness of body

Yes, health is part of wholeness, health is part of shalom. Sickness was no part of God's plan or intention for humanity; health and wholeness were. Wholeness, health of body, health of mind, health of heart and a whole health relationship between human beings and God. But shalom is more than personal wholeness, because we can't receive that in isolation. Shalom exists between persons where they have that relationship of love and unity which moves them both towards wholeness: shalom be between you and me. May we have the kind of relationship, the kind of trust, the kind of love, the kind of understanding, the kind of openness and honesty with each other, that our relationship is moving us both towards God's wholeness. God has placed us as human beings in such a way that we develop in our relationships with others - we each become unique persons because of our relationships to those around us and God's intention was that this should produce shalom.

Harmony, unity, trust, honesty, - more than that, shalom is a word used again and again in the Bible of God's intention for a neighbourhood, for a community, for a society and in that understanding shalom is that wholeness within a society where each person matters, each person is treasured, each person belongs and counts and is valued.

Shalom and justice

So, there is no shalom when one part of a society has its heel heavily down on the neck of another part. There is no shalom in a society of injustice. There is no shalom in a society where racism prevails. There is no shalom in a society of elitism and privilege and of the kind of unequal distribution of wealth that means that some people are living in dire poverty, while others live it up on beds of ivory.

And this is a message that we are not proclaiming today. The prophets did, Jesus did, the apostles did, but we have fallen silent because we as God's people today are implicated in injustice. We are up to the neck and over involved in injustice. We sit here, probably all of us, as representatives of 'man's inhumanity to man' and we don't say boo to it. We are the beneficiaries of injustice and we tolerate that situation, and as God's people we have not been active in the pursuit of justice.

The parts of our Bible which will probably have no underlining whatsoever are God's clear commands to pursue justice: 'That's not our message, we're evangelicals. There are other people who are interested in that.' It is God's message. God's message is for shalom and justice. 'And shalom and God's purposes will kiss each other'; 'Justice will roll down like a river.' So we cannot ignore God's call to shalom that involves justice.

There are prophets who say 'shalom, shalom' when there is no shalom. There are false prophets and the false prophets of the Bible identified stage after stage with the status quo. They said the things that pleased the people in authority. The prophets of God spoke God's truth. When God's heart was hurting, they expressed that hurt and when God was angry, they expressed God's anger. And we dare not sing these happy songs if we are not at the same time to share the hurt of the world and the hurt in God's heart.

I put it to you that a discipleship which is a discipleship in the Spirit of God is one which is concerned with the things which concern God's heart. We'll find ourselves returning to this one if we're going to stay with God's word.

We could go further. Shalom is taken right out into the whole created order. Job says that the very beasts of the field shall be in shalom and Isaiah gives us a vision - I wonder if it's just a dream, or is it really a vision that will come about? I dare to hope so. I wonder if I'm a sentimentalist. I have wondered again and again about animals, again and again about the little dog to whom we told so many of our troubles; who was God's means again and again of bringing healing when we were disturbed; who at points of loneliness and friendlessness was the one thing that God gave us to bundle around in life.

I wonder about the solitary, lonely people whose lives God has caught up with another part of His creation. Certainly Isaiah gives us a vision that the lion and the lamb shall lie down together and a little child shall lead them. Perhaps it's just a dream pointing us to the reality that will come, but one dares to hope that God does mean to, through Jesus, to bring us a whole creation restored in Him - and will do do.

The Prince of Shalom

Let's move quickly to Jesus, the centrepoint of the whole of history, of God's purposes for His world. In Isaiah again we have these words, looking forward to the one who is to come: 'Unto us a child is born, unto us a son is given, his name shall be the Prince of Shalom.' The one who is to come shall be the Prince of Shalom, and Isaiah adds 'and of his government and of his shalom there will be no end.' So, over Bethlehem, whatever else we make of the song of the angels: 'Glory to God in the highest, on earth shalom.'.

So as we look through the ministry of Jesus we find again and again as He approaches people: 'Your trust has made you whole. Go into shalom.' As Jesus reached out and brought healing to the deaf man, healing to the blind, fitness to the person whose limbs had been disjointed, forgiveness to the person whose life had been screwed up by guilt, He said 'Go into shalom.' Each healing was an indication that the King was present, that the reign of shalom, the reign of wholeness had come among human beings. And each healing was a sign of the total wholeness, the full shalom that is God's will for His world. In John's gospel, the very word that we translate as miracles - semeion - is the word for a sign. Each miracle was a sign of the presence of the Messiah, the presence of the King, the presence of God's reign, the presence of the wholeness, the healing, the fulness that was God's purposes for us. You'll find one reference there - Mark 5:34 - if you want to chase it along.

The place of shalom
Jesus' ministry moved towards one goal, towards the cross. Isaiah had said of the Messiah, 'the chastisement of our shalom was upon him.' (Isaiah 53:5) The chastisement that is the means of bringing us to God's wholeness was upon Him. As He died that death upon the cross, Jesus was doing something on the part of the broken world that we could not do for ourselves. As the one shalom man, the one whose whole body, heart, mind was as God intended it to be, the one who was wholly right with God, wholly right with those around Him, wholly right with the created world, the Messiah Himself, offered Himself for our world upon the cross. By His stripes we are healed. The Prince of Shalom gained shalom for us upon the cross.

Paul puts it this way in Colossians 1:20, 'He has made shalom through the blood of His cross.' 'But the God of shalom raised Jesus from death,' Hebrews 13:20. And Jesus at that last supper fulfilled the promise of the Old Testament to create a new covenant of shalom, a covenant in His blood, and we become the people of shalom. We'll look at this another evening, but just note in passing - when Paul speaks in Ephesians of Jews and non-Jews being divided by a wall of alienation he says that Jesus, by His death, has smashed down the dividing wall and from these two is making one new humanity, thereby creating shalom. And those of us who are caught up by Jesus Christ in this new peoplehood are empowered by God's Spirit, enabled by God, to be the new people of shalom, demonstating the very reign of God in the midst of a broken world.

And it's that kind of challenge that God is placing upon us. We are called upon, in the midst of an old order, to live as the people of the new order, the people of the shalom.

So, as we gather to the Lord's Supper we have the kiss of shalom. It's been restored in some of our liturgies as a little handshake, but in the early church it was a glorious affirmation of brotherhood, sisterhood: people found their way to each other and enthusiastically embraced each other because of the new social reality that God had brought into being through Jesus Christ.

As black man and white man hugged one another, something new had come into the world, because of Jesus. As the Roman matron who'd become a Christian, the Jewish streetgirl who'd been a prostitute, who'd found new life and love in Jesus, hugged one another, something new had happened. And we dare not come to the Lord's table unless we understand the nature of the new family, the new humanity of which the kiss of shalom is a symbol and a sign and a sacrament.

The makers of peace

What does it mean that Jesus says, 'Blessed are the makers of shalom'? Blessed are the peacemakers - yes? Blessed are the makers of shalom, the people whose lives under God, open to His Spirit, are committed to the pursuit of wholeness in all its manifestations. Does it do anything for us to look to the end of God's vision and to recognise that when God tells us that to the earth comes down from God the new Jerusalem, (Jerusalem is Jeru and shalom: the city of shalom) and that God's purpose is to bring into this Babylon His wholeness, His completeness, His perfection?

So God's vision is the bringing of wholeness and completeness to the whole of the creation that He loves. God so loved the cosmos - not just us, though we're important to God - but it's the totality of the cosmos which God so loved and for which He sent His Son. We miss a primary dimension of the gospel if we ignore the fact that the whole of creation is groaning in travail, but is going to come to new creation, because of Jesus.

We also need to remember that the Spirit was there at the first creation, the Spirit was responsible for the incarnation, the Spirit responsible for the resurrection, the Spirit responsible for the new creation. It's God's Spirit who's responsible for the hush in some of our hearts just now, as we realise we're facing something of God.

Entering the kingdom

Time is going. Let me simply draw one little picture that the Bible gives us of wholeness and let's not lose sight of the fact that shalom is the content of God's reign and that Jesus came proclaiming the good news of God's reign. In fact, you'll find it neatly put for you in Acts 10:36, 'God is making known the good news, shalom through Jesus, He is Lord of all.' Shalom through Jesus, He is Lord of all.

But there are some words that are related to this that might awaken us perhaps. Jesus said, 'How hardly shall a rich man enter the kingdom of God.' These are dreadful words from Jesus - dreadful to those of us who live in the West, knowing what we're doing to the people of the Third World; dreadful to those of us in the West knowing the situation of so many others who are not as we are.

When did you last hear that preached? Jesus says, 'Woe to you who are rich now,' do you hear those words upon His Body today? Does the Body of Jesus open its lips to say words like those to the world? In our evangelistic campaigns, the people who come down to the front, who long to respond to Jesus Christ, do we stop them and say, 'Woe to you who are rich now"? Are we faced with the demands of the new order in the presence of the old? Or do we call people to some kind of easy gospel that is no gospel, that says, 'Live the life of the old order and Jesus will give you peace while you do it'? Is that our message?

The disciples who responded to the words of Jesus when He said, 'How hardly shall a rich man enter the kingdom of God', with 'who then shall be saved?' You see, to enter into the kingdom of God is to be saved and salvation as a concept is linked up with shalom and linked up with the kingdom of God. It's a word of emancipation, a word of liberation, a word of freedom.

That which is saved is brought from a situation of un-freedom into a situation of freedom, from a situation of unwholeness into one of wholeness. And it covers all kinds of situations: the disciples in the storm at sea turned round and cried, 'Lord, save us!' Yes, they were in a situation from which they wanted deliverance into security. To people who were lacking in health, Jesus says, 'Your trust has saved you.' Yes, salvation has to do with the healing of broken bodies and yes, of course, it has to do with the restoration of the friendship and love between God and ourselves for which He has been longing, for which He has done all that needs be done to call us to trust.

So salvation is a concept of liberation into wholeness. The Old Testament word - some of you may know this already, if you don't, it's a fun thought - the Old Testament word means to take out of confinement and constriction into something that's open. The Old Testament verb 'to save' was to take out of a situation where people were being squeezed!

And having been released we can rejoice. The word chairein, which is the verb which we translate rejoice, comes from char. And char is the root that means well-being - very close to wholeness, and charis is that attitude within one person which moves out to pursue the well-being of another. The charis of God is God's longing in His heart that you experience wholeness, God's longing that you have total well-being. And chara - joy - is your experience of God's well-being.

Joy - how hard it is to find a word that says what joy means - is our experience of the well-being, the wholeness that God has brought us. And charisma, if I dare say it in this gathering, is that which arises from God's charis, that which is the outcome, that which is the result given to us by the charis of God.

Messiahed in the Spirit

I'm almost going to stop. I want to draw attention once again to what we read right at the beginning. Jesus when He stood up in the synagogue said, 'The Spirit of the Lord is upon me because He has anointed me.' I'm going to suggest that some of you might find this a fruitful thought - I'm going to make up an English verb from the noun messiah, the verb to be messiahed. It doesn't exist as far as I know, but you see, the Hebrew word messiah is the Greek word christos or Christ, and that, in English is the word anointed.

And I find it very sad that so many people can read the New Testament and, because of our translations, not realise how often the apostles are talking about the Messiah. The word Christ is not a surname for Jesus. It's not His second name, it's a title - Jesus Messiah. And all the meaning of the whole of the Hebrew vision is caught up in that. Paul says that, 'I have decided to know nothing among you except Jesus Messiah and Him crucified.' Also notice that Jesus was messiahed in the Spirit. It's by the Spirit of God that messiahship takes place.

And as an almost final thought, because this takes us into tomorrow evening, to be in Christ is to be in the Messiah. To be christianoi, which is what they were first called at Antioch, is to be messiah people. And to be anointed in the Spirit is to be messiahed in the Spirit. And if by trust you have placed yourself by God's grace within the kingdom of God, you are a messiah person, and a member of the Messiah people and you are caught up by the Spirit of God with the Messiah to be with Him all that God called Him to be, in bringing of the world to God's shalom.

The very last thought. It was a message of the reign of God that Jesus brought to the people, and with it the challenge to repentance. And repentance is not some kind of wishy-washy regret. Repentance is not sitting down for half an hour in tears. Repentance is the very thing which changes the total orientation of our lives, our total outlook: metanoia means a change of attitude, a change of orientation, a change of understanding and the totality is changed. Have we experienced repentance? Jesus called people to repentance and then to enter into the kingdom.

It is my prayer that any of us who are outside of the kingdom during these few days will, in the love they experience within this community, move into the kingdom. It is my prayer that those of us who have been in the kingdom will understand what we're in and will look to the Spirit of God to empower us to be what we are in Christ.

Let's pray.

The Messianic People

A new people

Some lines from Peter first of all. Reading in the first chapter, the second verse - Oh, why not read it all? They must have had much faster meetings in the early church when they had one scroll up front! I think we should pay attention to that - to how the gospel was spread by people who didn't have copies of God's word, but had hid it in their heart; where families sat together for hours and hours memorising very precious documents that had to be passed on to others. And that memorising and that hiding in their hearts was something that they needed to do at a time when persecution overtook them, as it did so soon.

'Peter, an apostle,' a missionary, one sent out, that's what the word apostle means, one who is on mission. 'Peter, one who is on mission, for Jesus Messiah to the exiles of the dispersion in Pontus, Galatia, Cappadocia, Asia and Bithynia, chosen and destined by God the Father and sanctified by the Spirit for obedience to Jesus the Messiah and for sprinkling with His blood.

'May grace and shalom be multiplied to you. Blessed be the God and Father of our Lord Jesus Messiah; by His great mercy we have been born anew to a living hope through the resurrection of Jesus the Messiah from the dead, and to an inheritance which is imperishable, undefiled and unfading, kept in heaven for you, who by God's power are guarded through faith for a salvation ready to be revealed in the last time.

'In this you rejoice, though now for a little while you may have to suffer various trials, so that the genuineness of your faith, more precious than gold, which though perishable is tested by fire, may redound to praise and glory and honour at the revelation of Jesus the Messiah.

'Without having seen Him you love Him. Though you do not

now see Him, you believe in Him and rejoice with unutterable and exalted joy. As the outcome of your faith you are obtaining the salvation of your total beings.

'The prophets who prophesied of the grace that was to be yours searched and enquired about this salvation. They enquired what person or what time was indicated by the Spirit of the Messiah within them. When predicting the sufferings of the Messiah and the subsequent glory, it was revealed to them that they were serving, not themselves but you, in the things that have now been announced to you by those that proclaimed the good news to you through the Holy Spirit sent from heaven, things into which angels long to look.

'Therefore, gird up your minds, be balanced. Set your heart fully upon the hope that is coming to you at the revelation of Jesus the Messiah. As obedient children do not be conformed to the passions of your former ignorance, but as He who has called you is holy, be holy yourselves in all your conduct since it is written "You shall be holy for I am holy".

'And if you invoke as Father Him who judges each one impartially according to his deeds, conduct yourselves with fear throughout the time of your exile. You know that you were ransomed from the futile ways inherited from your fathers, not with perishable things such as silver and gold, but with the precious blood of the Messiah, like that of a lamb without blemish or spot.

'He was destined before the foundation of the world, but was made manifest at the end of times for your sake. Through Him you have confidence in God who raised Him from the dead and gave Him glory so that your faith and hope are in God.'

The Good News
Again, thank God for His word. We needn't say more. Just a quick recap; I'll try to be as basic as I can. Someone said today that we are not really dealing with things that are anything other than basic. These are basic things we're talking about; we've actually been talking together about the very most basic things of the good news and I apologise if my training and the fact that I love reading and catch on to words quite quickly, if that has meant that for some people a number of words haven't gone home, and that's halted you from time to time. I apologise for that.

So, let's try tonight to say the same things and to say them a little more clearly. Perhaps by saying some of them now three or four times we'll catch on together.

I've been suggesting that one of the exciting things that God's

Spirit is giving us today is a fresh understanding of the good
news itself, something as basic as that; but at that, at the very
basic level of what the good news is, God's people have chosen
or whatever, to misunderstand. The good news is good news of
Jesus, of God's love from all eternity, pursuing humankind and
the whole creation, to restore what has become broken and estranged
both from Himself and from each other, to restore them to wholeness
and completeness.

In His purposes, His Son, Jesus, came among us as fully human
and entered into the total life of humankind, and of humanity
in relation to the rest of creation. But He came as one, as the
Son of the Father, who was in no estrangement; He was not cut
off, He was not alienated from His Father; His life was one of
completeness and wholeness; that wholeness is given to us again
and again in Scripture as shalom and Jesus was the embodiment
of shalom.

He offered this shalom to others, demonstrated it in His relationships,
even with the storm on the lake, even with the loaves and fishes.
He brought shalom to others in His healings, in the forgiveness
that He gave and the new life that welled up, in the love that
He gave to people whose lives had been lonely and lost and without
love and in His attack on death.

There's one way of looking at the whole of the gospel as
a challenge by life upon death and all the manifestations of death,
of which disease and sickness and selfishness and greed and injustice
are symptoms. These are symptoms of death, they are making for
death. And life itself in Jesus confronted death, went through death,
overcame death and in His resurrection declared the triumph of
God's life over all the demonic forces.

But Jesus as Messiah was anointed by God's Spirit and it
was by the anointing of God's Spirit that Jesus moved among
people with love, with power and doing good. And Jesus brought
into being around Him, those who were to form the nucleus of
a new humanity, which they were to be made capable of being,
because they, too, would be anointed by God's Spirit. To be a
new humanity means to be men and women and young people
whose total lives and relationships and values are remade by the
Spirit of God. In other words, Jesus brought into being God's
reign and asked us who are His followers, His brothers, His sisters
- He asked us to be the new humanity, giving evidence of the
reign of God: that God is king; that Jesus is Lord; that history
is His; that life has meaning, has purpose; that each individual
person matters, has value and is loved of God; and that death

is not an ultimate reality, because life in Jesus has conquered death. And this new people is called to be a new order living in the midst of the old.

The Body of Christ

Many people have asked me questions - and some of them I am going to take away and think seriously and do further research. That's one of the ways in the Body we can help each other: get at the people who have access to things you don't have. They are part of the Body, you have a right to ask of them. I have absolutely no right to the privilege of a theological education and all that lies with that unless that is available to the Body. You have no right to your training in economics, or to your training in an office, or as a homemaker, if that's not available to me. All right? So let's use each other. We're small enough, those of us who have this vision.

I have asked us, please, in our reading of the New Testament, to recognise that the name Christ is not a surname, but a title and I find that that makes a shattering difference to my reading of the New Testament. I don't know if when I've been reading to you and substituting 'Messiah', if that has that made a difference? The very fact that it arrests our attention and breaks the natural train of our thought means that we have to pause.

Just a few texts. 'We are proclaiming the Messiah, crucified', 1 Corinthians 1:23; 1 Corinthians 5:7, 'the Messiah is sacrificed for us, our Passover'; Hebrews 9:28 , 'the Messiah was once offered to bear the sins of many'; 1 Peter 3:18, 'the Messiah died for sins, once for all; the man of justice for the men of injustice that He might bring us to God; being put to death in the flesh, He was made alive in the Spirit'; Romans 8:34, 'It is the Messiah Jesus who died, yea, rather, who was raised from the dead'; Romans 8:9, 'If any person has not the Spirit of the Messiah, he is none of His'; 2 Corinthians 5:17, 'If any person be in the Messiah he is a new creation'; Ephesians 4:32, 'God has forgiven you in the Messiah'; 1 Corinthians 6:15, 'Your bodies are members of the Messiah's'; 1 Corinthians 12:27, 'You are the body of the Messiah'; 1 Peter 4:13, 'You are partakers of the sufferings of the Messiah'; 2 Corinthians 1:5, 'the sufferings of the Messiah abound in us'; Hebrews 11:26, we read of the reproach for the sake of the Messiah; and in 2 Corinthians 3:3, 'you are the epistle of the Messiah'. In a time of no books, or perhaps in a time when books have taken over and there is a glut, you are the epistle, the letter of the Messiah.

2 Corinthians 5:20, 'we are ambassadors for the Messiah';
Revelation 20:6, 'priests of the Messiah'; Ephesians 6:6, 'servants
of the Messiah'; Romans 8:17, 'joint heirs with the Messiah'; Colossians
3:13, 'as the Messiah forgave you, so also you do forgive one
another'; 1 Corinthians 2:16, 'we have the mind of the Messiah'.
And this is beautiful: 2 Corinthians 10:1, 'the meekness and gentleness
of the Messiah.' 2 Corinthians 12:9, 'the power of the Messiah'.
I had great fun going through this. Ephesians 3:82 speaks of 'the
unsearchable riches of the Messiah.' We need have no fear of
voluntary poverty for his sake. This is an interesting one, 'the
sweet savour of the Messiah,' 2 Corinthians 2:15.

Going home

Now, we're going to have a little break and I'm going to start
us off by sharing together some of the difficulties that some of
us find in going home with this message. Now I have tried not
to be specific, can I explain why I have tried not to ground in
specifics the things I've been saying? One of the reasons is that
we're a very motley group here and the specifics of one would
be very different from the specifics of another. And for one group
to work at what another group could work at might be not of
God, almost certainly wouldn't be of God.

The group here who've got a community life have been together
for a long time, have learned a lot of pretty hard and pretty expensive,
but very valuable, lessons - are at a different place from those
of us who have come here for the first time from a totally different
kind of setting, where the gospel in terms of our relationships
is quite differently understood.

Some of us are going back in groups that can work at things
together, others are going back as individuals with an overwhelming
sense of it having been beautiful and enriching and really of God
to be here, but we're going home on our own. So there are the
things that one group could apply, while another group is at a
different place.

So I've tried to be responsive under God to something that
we will apply differently and tonight we're going to have to help
each other to take the first steps in whatever place we are. Now,
one of the questions that I want us to work through together to
set us off on that journey is 'What do we mean by being a messiah
people or a shalom people?' I don't mean just what I have said
it means, I'm not a guru. It may well be that the truth God
gives you may be different from the one that left my mind, as
I understood it. Often a person preaches and someone comes and

thanks them for preaching something that they've no recollection of talking about. God has an incredible way of using His word that way. Don't try to recapture or remember things that have come from this podium. Be responsive to what God has been saying to you and share 'What does it mean, what are we being asked to be, as God asks us to be a messiah people?' Let the dream, the vision catch hold of you. God's got the resources.

Koinonia

I want to share a few thoughts on what the New Testament means by koinonia: that's the word that's usually translated by the word fellowship. And there's a sense in which we can talk about the Messianic Fellowship, because this idea comes through a very good deal in the New Testament and in the early Christian church.

The English word has a fascinating beginning; fellow is a legal word and it actually means people who share the possession of property, though we can't carry that back into the Greek. Koinonos is the Greek word for a workmate, someone who shares with you in an activity, in an experience, in a piece of work, in a chunk of life. Koinonia is the experience of being a mate to someone else in life, in a piece of work. Mateship gets quite close to it. The Australians are keen on mateship, but it's not a word that we use much.

Koinonia is a word of participation, of activity, of co-operation, of joint involvement in something. It's not that kind of easy, unctiousness we sometimes get. Fellowship is participation, activity, involvement together. In some contexts it means joint life. James and John are called Peter's koinonia in the fishing business in Luke 5:10. They were partners; this was the thing they had their lives invested in together, literally. Paul describes Titus as his koinonos and co-worker when he's pleading for Onesimus. (That's a fascinating and beautiful story. Anyone who thinks the early church did nothing about slavery, have a close look at Philemon. When the slave who's gone off comes back, he's to be welcomed, not simply as a brother in the Lord, but as a brother in the flesh. In other words, the guy who'd been serving at table and washing feet and so on, is a person and sits down at table. In a Christian household, the whole concept of slavery: gone! reversed!)

The Pharisees deny that they have been koinonoi of those who killed the prophets, despite what Jesus said. And Paul doesn't want the Corinthians to become koinonoi of demons. It's possible, Paul says, to be caught up in a joint participation with the demonic.

Just one or two references. 1 John 1:3, 'our koinonia', our

partnership if you like, 'is with the Father and with His Son the Messiah'; 2 Corinthians 13:14, Paul prays for the Corinthians that they will have the koinonia from the Holy Spirit. And we see everywhere in the New Testament that the fellowship which they share and enjoy and the participation and activity and the mission and the service they're involved in together comes from God's Spirit.

So the Messianic People become a fellowship messiahed by the Spirit, are given fellowship by the Spirit and are sent into participation and service and mission by the Spirit. And I'm thrilled that we're going to sit down together at that feast. 'The cup that we drink,' says Paul, 'is it not a koinonia of the blood of the Messiah? The bread which we break, is it not a koinonia of the body of the Messiah?' And then Paul longs in Philippians 3:10, to 'know Him and the koinonia of His sufferings'.

1 John 1:7, 'If we are walking around in the light' - peripatein means walking around, moving around all the time - 'if we are walking around in the light, then we are having koinonia with each other and the blood of Jesus is decontaminating us.'

Hebrews 13:16, 'Don't be forgetful of koinonia for God is well pleased with such sacrifice.' Dwell on that one, those on whom that rests. And then 2 Corinthians 8:4, we see koinonia used in a very practical way; the communities in Macedonia beg the koinonia of the service towards the saints. In Philippians 1:4, koinonia used in the same way, of the joint participation we have of giving of our goods, giving of our substance, to help those brothers and sisters who are in desperate need, those who are in prison, those who are in poverty.

Paul thanks God for the Philippians and their koinonia towards the gospel from the first day until now. And for Philemon, straightening out his relationship with the one who had been his slave. Paul prays for him that the koinonia of his faith may become active for the Messiah. There's so much one could go on to.

Koinonia is such a constant, continuing experience of the life of the early church. Recognise it as koinonia with the Father and with the Son, recognise that we're called into the koinonia of the Son. Let's recognise that it's koinonia in the body and the blood of Christ. Let's recognise that it's koinonia that comes to us by the Spirit of God. Let's recognise that it's a covenant and contrast with the demonic. Let's notice that it's a koinonia that brings us into the sharing of the sufferings of the Messiah; it's a koinonia with God and it's a koinonia with each other. It's a koinonia on behalf of the world.

New wineskins

I want to move now to another question - and it may be that there are different people for whom these little snippets are intended. There are those of us who've been thinking with love for the congregations of which we're a part, and I trust that whatever may be the situation in which we know them to be, we do look upon them with love. It's very easy to find within our hearts very different feelings when we find ourselves thwarted in things that are clearly for us promptings of God's Spirit; but as soon as we do that we begin to stifle the Spirit, because we place ourselves out of fellowship.

So, in love let's recognise some of the realities. Some of us have got real difficulties with the use of the word 'church'. I haven't used the word church very much here; you've possibly been aware of that. It's been deliberate, because that word today has come to mean so many different things that it's almost ceased to be a code which communicates to people. And I would like very much if we could get rid of it altogether, because it's so confusing.

We have recognised clearly from God's word that what Jesus was building around Himself was a people. The church essentially and centrally is a living organism, people united in Jesus Christ, messiahed by His Spirit, gifted, energised by His Spirit. Now one of the metaphors that Jesus used for the new covenant people He was bringing into being was wine. He uses the metaphor that we are wine. Now God has never been without His wine; old Israel was wine and it was present in the world in wineskins, but Jesus recognised that the wineskins of the old covenant were inadequate for God's new wine, for His new people.

Now the wineskins are the things by which God's people are present to the world. There is no way that a living organism is without shape and without structure. Some of us have got an anarchist streak inside of us that is opposed to structure. That's crazy. Structure enables us to be present, to grow, to move and be energised. The question is: 'Have we got the right structure: is the organisation the right organisation for the organism?' This is a bit of a tough idea.

Let me put it another way. The wineskins are the kind of things that history makes. Every one of us in this tent at Post Green belongs to a kind of denomination, or has done. Those denominations came out of history at a particular time when a group of people wanted, for whatever reason, to be more true to

God's purpose as they saw it, with the people they were trying to reach. So a new shape grew up out of history. In a very short time these people believed that their shape went back to the apostles but it didn't. It was shaped by history. And that includes a whole lot of us who've got a very treasured heritage - they were all shaped by history.

A whole lot of the things that we take for granted today in our churches and believe that they go right back to Christ, are no older than Queen Victoria. And quite frankly, when she snuffed it, so should they. And we're landed with a whole lots of forms and a whole lot of things that were brought into being to give a particular expression to the gospel, to allow the gospel to be seen and experienced in a particular way. If you think of the different shapes of the church in the different parts of the world, we recognise that the cultures have shaped the particular forms that the church takes; even things like its liturgy, even things like the way its authority is structured, the way it sits in a church, or stands.

You can go to some parts of Scotland where people stand up for prayer and sit down for hymns. And there'd be no organ and they'd be appalled at the suggestion of an organ. That's a structure. A very large number of congregations sit the way we're sitting just now. Fortunately, we've got other ways of relating to each other. When we move around hugging each other, we can relate as God's people. But there are some congregations where the very fact that they sit in pews means there's a whole lot of things about the gospel that they can't do.

People come into a church with all kind of problems happening back home. Dad and Mum have not slept together for the last couple of years. There's a deep bitterness about it, not often spoken. The teenage son has been told to be in by 11 o'clock and he creeps in at 2.00 to find that Dad has not been asleep. The teenage daughter has been quarreling with mother all the way through breakfast and there's problems going on about her own identity. And that little foursome finds it way into the church, as neat as you like, and stands up with hymn books and the thing goes on from start to finish. They've said their good mornings, they say their goodbyes and there's nobody in that congregation who knows what's going on inside that family, the turmoil, the strife, the pain, the broken relationships. There's no healing brought to them, there's no opportunity for hugging.

Any possibility that they might need to weep together before God with brothers and sisters would be absolutely appalling. And as for the expression of exuberance and joy in the Spirit, well, we know what happens.

I'm not wanting to ridicule, I want us to love, but I want us to be realistic and recognise that some of us are going back with ideas, with understandings, with experiences that are going to be very strange to folks within our congregations and I'm suggesting to you that these are wineskins, they are not wine. The wine is the people of God, constantly being kept new by God's Spirit. But the wineskins are getting old, they are getting cracked. Some of them are fit to burst. We need wineskins; new wineskins, new structures.

There are to be administrators, there are to be evangelists, there are to be preachers, they are asked to stoke the boiler, they are asked to do an infinite number of things and to be totally available 24 hours a day. And the gifts that God means to be in the Body - one guy who has not got them all is trying to live as if he had. Now let's not be under any pretence. If the charismatic understanding of the people of God, which is central to the New Testament comes into its own, it will mean an end to clericalism and priestcraft. There is no question about it. And those of us who try to believe that the two can be held together, that some kind of tinkering around can be done which will allow us to remain with clericalism and still have an expression of the koinonia of fellowship, we've no understanding.

Now, how do we move from where we are now, recognising the wineskins in which most of us are placed, how do we function among brothers and sisters responsibly? God has given us responsibility along with new knowledge. How do we bring new light into that situation? I'm going to leave that problem with you in a few moments. But I'm going to suggest to you that structures which hide Jesus, which distort Him, which screw up the gospel are heretical. Structures can be heretical in that they shut people off from the power of the living Messiah and the wholeness He has to bring.

It's not simply another little thing that you happen to sit in serried rows and you stand and you kneel and you do this in a perfunctory way and that you have no possibility of relating to people in a deep meaningful way. That's not just incidental, it is heretical, because it is destructive of the wholeness that God, by His Spirit, longs to bring to His people. So we're not just talking about a new order for out there in the world, we're talking about an enormous thing we've got to pray for in God's Spirit, right among us. And some people have got channelled off into nice little fellowship groups in comfortable suburban lounges and

what they ought to be doing in the congregation they are not
doing, because they are allowed to do their little thing, stuck out
there in suburbia. And I would like to challenge that.

Re-creating God's people

Is the energy of God's Spirit being used to recreate His people?
In your small groups. I want you to try to identify what are the
problems in practical terms that we know we are going to have
to face, taking back home with us an understanding of the gospel
as about God's kingdom and of the Christian community as part
of the gospel, part of the good news? What are the problems?

In the last few minutes I'm quickly going to suggest one or
two things. Let me give a quick correction - my reference to clericalism
was not necessarily meant as a reference to clergy; my reference
to priestcraft was not necessarily to be interpreted as a reference
to priests. I think you'll realise there's a difference.

I think God's people always need people to enable us to exercise
the gifts God has given and to be the people of God. But those
clergy should place themselves thoroughly within the laity, which
is where they belong in the New Testament, they are part of the
laos of God, not priests in any way that others are not priests.

A missionary God

Just a few pastoral thoughts, since it's my last chance to speak
to the whole group. Let us place first and foremost in our minds
that God is God and Jesus is Lord and the messianic work we're
called into is one in which He is already and powerfully engaged.

Our God is a sending God, a missionary God. He doesn't
send us on a mission, He catches us up in His mission. We participate
with the mission of God, so there is no cause for fear or alarm.
It is His mission, He knows what He's about; He's engaged in
it; He's got the strategy; He's got the plan, all the resources and
all the love and He's prepared to make those available as we
are prepared to be His. So first of all, let's get that quite straight,
we serve a missionary God and we're entering into an eternal,
pursuing love.

Let's recognise that Jesus tells us to seek first the kingdom
and its justice and all things will be added. Other things will
follow, that's what He's saying.

Get your priorities right. Don't start working at these other
things until you're on a pursuit and a searching for the kingdom.
Seek first the kingdom and the other things will fall into their
place.

If there's one thing we've been trying together to do as a planning team, it's to help us to the kind of overview which allows us to see the nature of the kingdom, so that as we do our little bit under God, as we are obedient, we see our place in God's strategy and purpose as we move towards His vision. Don't allow yourselves the discouragement of expecting that somehow in your wee bit, the goal that God knows is coming, is going to happen with you tomorrow, jumping all the places you have to go to. Start. OK? Look ahead, but start and move at God's pace.

Then ask God for others to share the vision and the Body and the being with you. It is something that is a shared thing. From time to time God has had saints in very lonely places where they have been isolated, but God's purpose is not isolation, but that we be the Body in togetherness. However small the group, try to be part of a group of people who are working towards the kingdom, who are seeking the kingdom first with you. You may find they are in your congregation, you may find there's lone folk in other congregations; there may be some way of getting together and still staying loyal to the same congregations from which you come, if that's what God has called you to. But find people who will with you seek the kingdom of God first of all.

Be open under God to finding out where your own gifts under God lie; and to help others identify the gifts they have. God will help us to help brothers and sisters identify their gifts and how those gifts can be used, in the Body and outside of the Body.

So let's identify the gifts we have. Paul had to say to a young disciple, 'Stir up the gift that is within you.' It's a crying shame, but there are gifts present in this tent tonight in an abundance that are not being used. God's got all the resources He needs for His task, but they are stuck away under lock and key in your life and they are not available to Him. He's handed them out, He's waiting for them, they're needed - and they're locked up! Stir up the gift that is within you. Open up your life to the Spirit of God.

In this tent tonight there are a lot of fearful people, there are a lot of people who are shy to the point of inability. As I've moved around the camp site I've seen shyness and withdrawal. There is a shyness that's politeness, it's not brash or pushy. There is a shyness that is inhibiting and from which we need to be released and it is not a kindness to a brother or sister to leave them in a situation which is not released and is not free. And some of us who know that we are held back by an inhibiting shyness must open those areas to the Lord. There are deep, deep hurts within us and within every human being. Some of us by ourselves will never track down the source. Perhaps it's not important to; to track down things that have happened way, way back as we've been growing, that have inhibited us, set us on a track that has not been a wholesome one.

Open our lives to God's healing, become free, become buoyant. Claim one little area that you can handle for God. Begin your mission, your service, your caring in an area that, under God, you and the others around you can handle together. Don't be appalled by the misery around. Weep for it, but take on something you can handle and which, under God, you can see change. Take on one family, two families. Pray for them, get to know them. Be concerned for their relationships, take responsibility for the lives of others.

Open to each other
It's totally un-British to take responsibility for anybody else's life. It's totally un-British to allow anyone to have responsibility for ours. But when we've done it, the freedom and the feeling and the release that comes is worth all that it costs.

I learned today that if it's un-British, it's even more un-Swedish and I wouldn't have believed that. Our brothers and sisters told us today that in Sweden one thing they do not do is to hug or touch each other. All the stories I get from Sweden suggest something quite different!

But they shared with us that the most radical thing they could do is to go back as brothers and sisters who hug each other. The opening of our lives to God, the claiming of the lives of others, the sharing of the responsibility, taking up responsibilities for each other's life. I don't mean prying and poking. I mean really being responsible as we are for our own families whom we love. I mean authentically weeping as we do when something has happened in our own family. Really giving the time that it takes that we would give to somebody in our own family.

Many a Christian guy, who's had no time for kids who get in trouble with the law, suddenly realises what happens when his own son is up against it. The whole thing changes.

Have you noticed that the people who are at the heart of organisations for cancer research or for spina bifida are people whose families have suffered through these things? If God's people would suffer where they should be suffering, we'd be at the forefront of the things seeking healing.

Open to the Word
Study, and I say this with diffidence, because I find that easy
and I find it exciting. When I really want to be relaxed before
I get to sleep at night, I actually read Greek. I'm claiming nothing
by that. I'm going to suggest that perhaps the same should be
true for you; that God's going to need more and more people
who are able to handle His word.

I find it quite terrifying, the responsibility that I'm given each
time I use a word as it is in Greek. The authority I am claiming
and am given by brothers and sisters is very frightening. But there
is so much in our translating that has come through our culture
and so much of that culture that has been of the old order that
people quite unwittingly have brought across all manner of things
that don't allow us to see with sharpness what God is saying
to us today. You can learn Greek in six months, working on your
own. Or if you're less conversant with language it might take
a bit longer. I'm not suggesting that we'll all need to, but there
are some of you who are interested, already awakened and excited
who should be spending some time grappling with this. You'd
find it a joy, however much a labour. I'm just about to take in
Hebrew sufficiently to grasp what God is saying.

Let's handle God's word with confidence. When I was seventeen,
people knew their Bibles! We do not know our Bibles today. If
you were stuck in a prison cell somewhere, how much scripture
have you got to feed you if you don't have access to this book?
We do not know our Bibles. The Bible was never given to us
as a piece of devotional reading, for us to make a T S Eliot
out of the pages, so that we turn it into some kind of little exercise
that gives us a little glow inside. God's word will give us a glow
when we're being obedient, when it's speaking of Christ.

There's far too much Christian writing about God's word that
turns every specific of statement of God that requires obedience
into something that suddenly becomes a metaphor and is easy.
Juan Carlos Ortez draws our attention to those parts of our Bible
which are not underlined. 'Come unto me all you who are weary
and are heavy laden, and I will give you rest.' That's underlined,
right? Marvellous promise. Do you know how it goes on? 'Take
my yoke upon you.' Can we have the one without the other? I
can't see apart from God's word, how we develop the mind of
the Messiah.

Open homes, hands and hearts

There's so much I want to say, I'm going to throw it all together. God's people need to rediscover what it is to practise hospitality and to be beautiful in the way we are home makers for friends, for strangers. Far too few of us, for all the wrong reasons, are not open to brothers and sisters. We could have a work that was extended overnight and multiplied many times if we were prepared to open our hearts to God.

The early church didn't see their homes as their own, they belonged to God. They didn't choose the people who came and went, brothers and sisters passing round were always welcome. We need to rediscover hospitality. We're very bad in Britain. In America they have a good understanding, they know what it's about. I'm not just talking about Christian homes. Australia? Yes, they know in Australia. In Britain we are niggardly, we are beggarly. I don't know what's happened to God's people. How many people in your congregation have actually crossed your threshold? How many have been invited to a meal, or a time of fun. How many watch telly on their own when they could watch it with you?

I feel ashamed that people come across here now to visit Christians in Britain and it's hard to find people who're excited enough to welcome them. It's very interesting that the households that have a strong American influence have got a great deal more understanding of the practice of hospitality.

I was going to say something about creativity. Develop the talents God has given us. Start writing, writing poetry, start painting, making things, developing a love for God's creation; a real revelling in God's created order brings us an understanding of the Creator. It's very interesting that the people who appreciate creation most, appreciate the Creator. And the people who worship creation are not the ones who actually appreciate it. Prayer. I'd wanted to say something on that, but let's take that for granted.

We've been praying in the Spirit since we came here. Let's recognise that when Paul says we've to pray ceaselessly that he means the practice of the presence of God, where throughout the day, we offer situation after situation before it's come upon us to God; when we sit prayerfully in a bus or in a train, when we meet people and people leave us surrounded by our prayer; when people in our presence may not know it, but are being prayed for. I don't think that's improper. Do you think it's improper to pray for people without their knowing it? I do it all the time. Let's practise what it is to pray.

I find it hard now to come together for formal prayer. Maybe that's something I'm going to have to work at. It's becoming easier to practise prayer as a continuing conversation with God, that means a two-way thing, of being open to Him as well.

Open to mission
Somebody suggested that some of us may have to think very seriously about our jobs, about our houses; very seriously about the plans we've got for the future; very seriously about the areas of the country that are deprived of Christian presence. I can't believe that it is of God that all the Christians have had a vocation to go out into suburbia. Something has gone wrong; how did all the Christians get called out to the nice areas? It's very odd.

How is it that there are whole tracts of our cities without a Christian presence at all, the neediest areas. How is it that whole new towns go up, whole new housing areas go up, without a Christian presence? Yet, there's a glut of leadership in Bible belts all over the country, with so many leaders that congregations are constipated. They don't know what to do. They can't exercise the gifts of the Spirit because the gifts they've been given are not intended in that congregation. And some of us run around at preaching stations that we're needing to take more seriously than we do. Does God mean that to be how His Body is being built up?

Some of the most successful churches around the country in terms of numbers are doing so at the expense of little local presences of Christians. There is no Christian presence in some areas because all the folk are getting in their cars and driving an hour away to where they get fed. Do they get fed, if they're not being told to get back to where they come from and be a Christian presence there? They're not being fed, they're being entertained. Now that may mean some of us here. I'm not saying anything negative about the great men and women of God that He's raised up. I'm talking about those of us who have turned them into idols and who have missed out on the understanding of what it is to be a Christian presence where God has placed us. It may be that we do need a time for what we've had here, what some of these little oases across the country can give to people.

I don't think every one is called by God to the inner city. But I think a big percentage more are called than go! I think we'll stop there; I think we've got a picture, even if it is a messy one. A picture of the kind of things that we're working at. Above all, let's not get harassed - the demonic would be thoroughly happy if they thought they had us in disarray because the picture looked too big, the task looked too great. The task isn't too great at all. In God's time, with all of us doing our little bit - it might be a big bit for some of us!

Here's another thought that I've been shoving along for a little while. I believe that we're in a new missionary era of the Holy Spirit. I believe the things that God did when He thrust women and men out of very comfortable positions - of prestige in Britain and other parts of the world, out into needy areas across other continents to live in a way that nobody back home understood. We have no idea what people went across to, to live in a little village, where they hardly understood the language, where there was no sanitation, no school for the kids - they had to start one! No hospital for thousands of miles - they had to be the only hospital - and none of the securities of the old order that we take for granted. It was their faithfulness under God that brought the gospel and the healing and the light for which people have rejoiced since.

I believe that right now in Europe and in America, a comparable call is coming to men and women to cross cultural barriers they never knew existed and to relate to the ordinary people in our countries in a new way. Perhaps not just to the people who've grown up in our countries, but for the folk who have come among us and who are new British, who've come from other parts of the world. Could it be God's strategy that the people from Asia who are now living in Britain, catching the gospel, could go back to Asia with the gospel where we couldn't? People are now living in Britain from parts of Africa where the gospel is not strong. Could it be that if we were true to the gospel here that God has a different strategy today in a changing world? Could it be that in this tent God has got missionaries who are being called in a profound way to give up prestige, to give up success, to give up wealth, to give up security?

It's certainly my hope and my tremulous prayer that out of this gathering of God's people will come many, many, whose lives will be totally His, not in a rapturous un-grounded way, but in a way that would earth us in human hurt with the only message of healing, 'messiahed by the Spirit'.

Let's pray.

The Messianic Mind

The people of shalom

Let's begin this session with the promise in God's word, Psalm 29, verse 11, 'The Lord will bless His people with shalom.' We've already looked at 'The Messianic Vision'; we looked last night at 'The Messianic People' and we're going to look tonight - if God wills - and I don't crack before it because I've been broken already this evening - at 'The Messianic Mind' - at the attitudes, at the values, at the behaviour, at the motivation, that comes to us of God's Spirit as we are in the Messiah.

We looked at God's love, eternally longing to bring His creation to wholeness and moving in His Son towards the achieving of that wholeness. We looked at the promise that came down the ages, of shalom through the Prince of Shalom, who came at Bethlehem and moved to the cross, to the resurrection and to God's right hand. We looked at Him as the one who was messiahed in God's Spirit and we saw Him as the bearer of shalom, as the shalom man, complete in Himself, complete in His relation to God's creation, as the one who created it, through whom and in whom and for whom it was made; as the shalom man who was in the right relationship with the world around; as the shalom man who offered in His relationships with others only shalom. We saw Him as the one who in Himself was an embodiment of perfect humanity and of all that God calls us to be and intends us to be and has promised that in Christ we shall be. We looked at Him as the one who, by His cross, creates shalom for us with God, and rising again has returned to us, to move among us as He did among the disciples on the eve of His resurrection when His first word to them was 'Shalom'.

And so we find ourselves the Messianic people, messiahed in

the Spirit of God to be the bearers of shalom in a broken world
and to a fallen creation. We find ourselves called upon and enabled
by the Spirit to be the embodiment of shalom, the avante-garde
of the new creation, demonstrating the reign of God.

Constantine and compromise

For close on three hundred years, the Christian community struggled
to be true to being the Messianic people and being a new nation
within the old nations. However, as time passed towards the reign
of the Roman Emperor Constantine, things began to change quite
drastically and God's people, yet again, became unfaithful and moved
towards compromise and accommodation. They moved towards new
associations and an idolatrous respect for the old order and the
principalities and powers that lie behind it.

We can understand that if we think of the suffering that they
had gone through, of the persecutions they endured, of the loved
ones that they lost, of what they were put through as they were
prepared to be men and women of the new order in the presence
of the old; as they refused to bow the knee to Caesar and acknowledge
him as kurios, as lord, when there only is the one Lord - Jesus
Christ. And rather than deny Him, they went to the cross, they
were taken to the block and decapitated, they were dipped in tar,
stuck on stakes and set alight to give a glow to the emperor's
gardens when he entertained his guests. They were thrown to beasts,
they were compelled to fight against gladiators, they were drowned,
they were burned, they were mutilated.

We forget that the vision that John gives us comes from the
island of Patmos, where he was a prisoner for Christ in exile.
We forget how many of the Lord's apostles met death at the hands
of the old order and we forget that they met it because they were
obedient to Christ. So we can understand if things got terribly
tough and people got terribly tired. But it cannot excuse us, because
God's Spirit of love and God's Spirit of power was available then,
as it had ever been, and we are without excuse because we continue
in idolatry and compromise and we are in no position to pass
judgement.

Up until the time of Constantine there were many different
faiths abroad in the Roman empire competing against one another
- the Christian faith was simply one of these. Constantine's mother,
Helena, seems to have been a rather strange woman, but a woman
with some form of Christian convictions. She's the one who started
the original travel agency that went to the Holy Land. She was
the one who first established the places where all the relics were

supposed to be, she established where Jesus was supposed to have been born, and died - the places we still visit today are largely those that were determined by Helena - probably false, but we don't know.

But Constantine, on coming to power, decided that the easiest way to run his empire was to bring one religion to the whole of the empire. And he decided, without himself being a Christian, that it was in the best interests of himself and the empire that it be Christianity.

Up until that point, whether we like it or no today, Christians had refused to go to war in the interests of the old order. We know of the number of soldiers who were martyred when they became Christians and withdrew from military service that was other than policing. But from the time of Constantine, the Roman armies marched across the empire with a large cross in front of them. Something had happened to the gospel of Jesus and the message of shalom. There was a compromise at that time between the church and the state; and Christians of consequence and power were prepared to allow the gospel to retreat till it only dealt with private areas and did not challenge the structures and values of society. It became a private, personal religion.

So, instead of having little parliaments or embassies of the kingdom of God dotted everywhere, working through their responsibilities as agents of the kingdom of God, churches became little representations of the mystery religions. They took over from the mystery religions their robes, a great many of their lilting songs; as they crossed through Europe, they took over practice after practice from paganism. They couldn't get rid of the worship of Saturn on the 25th December so they made it the birthday of Jesus. They couldn't get rid of the worship of Astarte so they made it Easter. They couldn't get rid of the worship of the mother of God, the pagan fertility goddess, so they made her Mary. These are but little symptoms of what happened as the vibrant, vital faith of the New Testament community became a civil religion that lost the power of God's Spirit to change men's lives and cultures and the new order became an agent of the old order.

Perhaps you might find it interesting to reflect on one of the things that happened then - men and women and young people who were not prepared to compromise the gospel in that way retreated from that compromise into communitarian communities, households, farms, that became the earliest of the monastic communities. In fact, the monasteries grew up as a radical protest against the emasculation of the gospel of Christ. They didn't remain untouched by it, but we can praise God that through the period of the Dark Ages it was in those communities that God preserved the light of the Gospel. God preserved His word and it was from those communities that the word again emerged to transform and to bring us back to an understanding of the faith of the New Testament.

I've said that at length because I believe it's important again in our day that we understand this and why God is calling us to the kind of commitment to which we know in our hearts He's calling us; why men and women are being called once again into community life; why we're being called once again into the sharing of possessions and the sharing of lives and a new understanding of what that means.

Could it be that ahead of us - perhaps almost on top of us, unknown to us - is a compromise of the Christian faith by churches to which we would long to be loyal and for which we must give thanks to God for what they have given to us of the Good News of Christ? I put that forward simply as a challenge; it's one that has disturbed me for quite some time.

Marbles and honeycombs

The mind of Christ. I'd like to read a couple of passages from God's word. First of all from Ephesians in the second chapter, reading from verse 13 to verse 19. (I'd love to read the whole of Ephesians). When we come across the word Christ I'm going to use, with your permission, the word Messiah. (reads Ephesians 2:13-19) The second passage is in Philippians, from chapter 1, from verse 27 through to chapter 2, verse 15. (reads Philipians 1:27-2:15) I need hardly go on to say more. I don't apologise for those lengthy readings from God's word. 'Let this mind be among you which is also in Messiah Jesus.' Before we pass that, let's just note the ending of that reading from Philippians: it's an example of what I was suggesting to you yesterday, of where a command from Paul in the plural is to be seen as addressed to the whole community of God's people. If we all see ourselves only as individuals, we fail to understand that God by the Spirit has made His purpose possible.

Let me give this example. In a little book called 'Culture, Class and Christian Beliefs', John Bennington has this little illustration. He suggests that as Christians, (I've been corrected that we're not all evangelicals and I almost used that word just now) certainly as Christians in the Western world, we have got into the habit of privatising the gospel and believing that the gospel is directed to individual persons, mattering to God and being valued by Him in a private way.

If you doubt that, just look what happens at the Lord's Supper. All our heads go down one after the other in a private way. If you did that at an ordinary meal when you were invited out to a party, you'd be rude. And we're rude at the Lord's Supper when we don't discern the Body. It's not a private thing in which we all sit privately relating to one person.

John Bennington suggests this little analogy for what we have made of God's care for the individual. He suggests that we regard the individual like one of so many marbles in a box; remove one marble and the others go on, put more in and they just jostle around. The rest are not affected by the removal of one, because each marble is complete in itself. He suggests that that's the model from which we have been trying to live the gospel. You say, 'So what? It makes a lot of sense to me'.

Let's look at another analogy, which he suggests is more Biblical. Paul gives us one model in the Body, but we've become so accustomed to it that we don't hear it any longer, so John Bennington suggests the model of a honeycomb. Every cell in a honeycomb is unique and individual, but try to remove one of the cells in a honeycomb and you destroy something of six others, because the individuality which is there in the cell in a honeycomb is tied up with the individuality of those around it. And if that cell gets wrecked a bit of six others gets wrecked. And, in the body of Christ, if one member is weeping, six others should be in tears. If one cell is able to laugh there would be at least a ripple going round six sides.

Now that's the difference between the Bible's understanding of what it is to be an individual and the old order's understanding of what it is to be an individual; and it takes very little thought to realise which model our churches, and we ourselves, have been trying to operate for far too long.

So when Paul is addressing the churches in the New Testament and he addresses them in the plural, he's talking to honeycombs, he's not talking to marbles! And when he says 'Work out your own salvation with fear and trembling, for it is God who is at work among you,' he's talking about the community, together working out its wholeness, its movement into freedom, because it's God by His Spirit who is at work among them. He's not saying 'you A, you B, you C, go about your own thing; have your own personal quiet time and work out your own personal, individual, private salvation'. He's saying 'together work out your movement under God into wholeness'. It can be done together. It's how God means it to be done.

Repentance and holiness

The mind of Christ. Let this mind be among you. Let's link that with the word repentance. The word repentance means a change of mind, a change of heart, a change of attitude and outlook, a radical turn about of our understanding of what life is about, where life is going, what history means, what matters, what doesn't. And as we hear the message of God's kingdom - as a man, as a woman understands the message of God's kingdom, the realisation of what this is going to mean dawns on them. And it's the realisation of what this is going to mean that produces metanoia.

Metanoia is repentance and repentance is not a once and for all thing; repentance is something that must come to God's people again and again and again. There's a dynamic to repentance, as increasingly God brings the nature of the new order before us and challenges us, with His love and power, to move beyond into the new order to give further embodiment to the kingdom of God.

I love Isaiah 26:3: 'Thou wilt keep him in perfect peace, whose mind is stayed on thee.' The Hebrew has 'you will keep him in shalom shalom whose mind is stayed upon you.' Perfect peace is shalom shalom. And several times in the Old Testament we have this prayer from God's people or God's servants: 'Give to me a shalom heart.'

I was moved tonight because place after place in our singing, without it having been worked out, things God had laid on me came up. And as we moved through this evening, again and again I knew God was in what we are about tonight. We're here tonight in this place because God wants to have dealings with His people and God means things to be happening here. I felt broken because I myself sit under the very words that God gives me; it troubles me that God says of the one who teaches 'more is required' and I know how far short of the very word that God gives me to share I fall.

'Be not conformed to this age, but be transformed by the renewing of your mind.' (Romans 12:2) To be conformed to this age is to be caught up in the values and standards and hopes of the old order. To be transformed by the renewing of our mind is to allow God's Spirit to take over our hearts, our minds, our lives and make us men and women of the new order. And we're going to have to decide to let that happen daily. Perhaps you thought it was over when you decided for Christ and became a Christian. Built into this is a call to distinctiveness. The very metaphors that we've already referred to, that Jesus uses again and again, are metaphors of distinctiveness. His metaphor of salt, the salt is distinctive. It doesn't become the soil into which it is cast; it does not become the crap against which it is asked to stick; it remains distinctive. But God's people are to be found without distinctiveness today. We have become the soil and, God forgive us, we have become part of the crap. The word that we've lived with for a long time, (and it's an easy word to live with because it doesn't count much for us) the word holiness is the word for distinctiveness. The essential nature of holiness is distinctiveness and when God calls us to be a holy people He is calling us to be a distinctive people, a people whose lifestyle, whose relationships, whose values distinguish them from the old order.

I became a Christian at the point where the Christian community was very compromised with the old order. I became a Christian as a guy of almost eighteen, who had for many years been involved in dancing and enjoyed it. And I came into a group of people to whom the nature of worldliness was the fact that I enjoyed dancing. That was 'the world' for them.

Their homes were homes of luxury. The Christians I first met were moving towards success. They placed their top values on education, on popularity, on good families, on fine homes, on their sense of taste and dignity and culture. Those are of the nature of the world, those are the values and standards of the old order. And the demonic was thoroughly happy when we identified as the very nature of worldliness that someone smoked, that someone took a beer, that someone went to a dance, that a girl wore make-up. God forgive us.

It may be that for different people those are areas we've got to look at very seriously, but let's recognise how very much more subtly we have got caught up in the values and standards of the old order. And God's call to holiness is not a call to private goody-goodiness, it's a call to His people corporately, to a distinctive, identifiably distinctive, lifestyle, standards, values, in the midst of the old order.

Jesus and the old order
Jesus clearly rejected the options of the old order. Since we've nearly taken up our time, I won't go into these in depth, but just let's look quite quickly at what these were.

There was the option that was being offered to people by the Sadducees, the Jewish aristocracy, who had opened their homes to run cocktail parties for the Roman governors and their friends.

They were willing to be utterly compromised just so long as their own authority wasn't touched. From them came the high priests, who, in the time of Jesus, were actually appointed by the Roman governors. Perhaps that hasn't come to us before, they were actual appointments of Rome from the Sadducean families. This particular option we don't find attracting Jesus.

Then there were the Pharisees, men of very high morality, who had carried their morality to the point of moralism. And among us today, perhaps there are those who are not able to see the nature of ethical struggle because we've become moralistic. I ask you to think about that one - are we among those who would stone the woman taken in adultery? The Pharisees were the separatists, the ones who didn't want to be contaminated by the riff-raff; they were the academics, the lawyers, the ones who placed their major emphasis on a barren religion. Jesus was not attracted by that option.

There were the Herodeans. These were the monarchists who placed all their trust in the dynasty of the Herodean family. They were the right-wing nationalists; we've got them today too. Jesus was not attracted by that option. To those who came from Herod Jesus said, 'Go and tell that fox!'

Don't let anyone tell you that Jesus was soft politically; don't let anyone tell you that Jesus was not involved politically; don't let anyone tell you that Jesus was not a threat to the political forces of His time. If Jesus had not been a threat to the political forces of His time He would not have been crucified. Are we a threat to the political forces of our time? 'Oh, but they are Christian,' we say about the modern Herodeans. Are they?

Another option was the Essenes. An interesting group of radicals, who had taken themselves off into the desert where they had their private macro-biotic food places. They had their authentic rituals, without any accommodation with anything new. Things were done as they had always been done. They were strong pietists, people whom we must admire. It's even possible that John the Baptist was brought up among the Essenes. There are people among us today attracted by the Essene option, quite a number, but not Jesus.

There is nothing in the ministry of Jesus that we find attracting Him to identify with the Sadducees, Pharisees, Herodeans or Essenes, but there's one group that was a problem to Him. The church has been attracted by the Sadducees. Oh yes! Just look at the families from which our bishops have come for centuries. Just look at a state church, where very major decisions are made by politicians. The church is attracted to the Pharisees and their legalism. We can recognise it, perhaps some of us, inside ourselves right now. Yes, the Herodeans, we've been attracted by them and the Essenes. But here's the group that the church has never been attracted by - the Zealots.

The Zealots were a group drawn from the common people, a people's party. They were left wing nationalists and a dangerous crowd because they were really dedicated. They identified with ordinary people and were pursuing justice for the people. The problem there was that these were violent men, these were men of violence, men whose resentment and bitterness had turned them to hatred. It's fascinating to find that among the disciples of Jesus were at least two men who had been members of the Zealot party.

Most scholars seem to be agreed today that Judas Iscariot means 'Judas, the Dagger Man'. The Dagger Men were a small group of the Jewish resistance movement who acted as snipers, stabbing Roman soldiers as they caught them alone or just in twos. In all probability, Judas was a member of the resistance movement, who, for all he identified with Jesus, did not identify with the way of Jesus and harboured hopes right through those three and a half years that Jesus would yet turn out to be the kind of man that the Zealots wanted.

If we had time we could look at the temptations that Jesus faced and we could see the Zealot option was a real temptation for Jesus, because He loved the people. Jesus didn't go through un-real temptations - how dare we suggest it? And yet Jesus was tempted, tempted to violence, tempted to feed the poor. He saw them all round Him in their hundreds and their thousands and His heart was moved; it was a temptation to put Himself up on the pinnacle of the Temple and throw Himself down, which was the public expectation of what the Messiah would do when he came. Yes, Jesus was tempted because He loved people and He hated the injustice and He hated the poverty and He hated the homelessness. And to see women whose bodies couldn't even give suckle, couldn't give milk to their children, God's heart cried out. Jesus was tempted.

But you see, the way of Jesus is not the way of the old order and none of those options was acceptable, including the one that the church has very rarely been attracted to, (it's interesting, Jesus wasn't attracted by any of the ones that attract us) which Jesus rejected because the mind of Christ is not the way of violence and coercion.

The New Way
What then do we find as we look at the disciple group? (I'm
going to have to cut this bit right down!) We find a group of
men and women gathered around Jesus, freely, by choice, who
have joined Him through His invitation. We find Him commending
that they share with others and that they move around as a group
of sharing men and women. The answer, Jesus says, to human
sufficiency lies not in holding, not in weighing up treasures upon
earth. Instead, they were to be all together, His disciples, all the
apprentices of one master.

The word of Jesus must be heard: 'You are not to be called
master, for you are all brothers. Call no man father.' We have
got to work out in our time what that means. Even today within
a movement that is clearly of God there are signs of striving for
an authority that is beginning to look dangerous. We are not to
lord it over one another as those of the old order, Jesus makes
that very clear. Authority within the Christian community means
greater service, not superiority. The abandonment of privilege can
be seen among them. But to leave self behind - that doesn't mean
we are not to see ourselves as God sees us, to place the kind
of eternal value on our lives that God places, but we are to leave
behind the self-aggrandisement that pushes ourselves forward, that
desires some form of privilege.

We are to renounce wealth. Yes, I said, 'Renounce wealth'!
I can find no other way of dealing with the teaching of Jesus
than to say that Jesus required of His disciples that they renounce
wealth. It doesn't mean that they were not then allowed by God
to continue living in what they had been given by Him, but that's
a very different thing. 'You cannot,' said Jesus, 'serve God and
wealth.' He uses there the word mammon, believed to be a Syrian
word. 'You cannot serve God and mammon.' At one point Jesus
talks about mammon - it reads oddly in the Authorised Version
- the mammon of unrighteousness. What does that mean? -
unrighteousness is injustice and the mammon of unrighteousness
is the wealth that comes from injustice. And Jesus is quite clear
that, as we look to the world, the inequalities that we see in
terms of the resources in the world are a result of man's injustice
to man. And this one hurts us; other ones we can applaud, but
this one hurts. And we're going to wriggle. I find myself wriggling
at that one.

And we're to renounce reputation; among the values of the
new order is that we're not putting ourselves forward for recognition.
We're not seeking popularity. John drew attention a couple of mornings

ago to the devastation that has crept in amongst us as God's people in terms of the search of popularity and the pushing forward of popular figures.

Jesus has this to say to His disciples and He says it to us: 'Woe to you when all men speak well of you, for so did their fathers, the false prophets.' False prophets have always been spoken well of because they always tell us what we want to hear. The kings who were out of line with God's will valued the false prophets, because the false prophets confirmed the kings in what they were doing.

The true prophets suffered the consequences of being true to God. And there's a sense in which we buy popularity - and we can do it today - at the expense of the gospel. It's incredible how many of us working for Christian agencies find there are things we dare not say and cannot put into print, because, if we do, we get letters in the next mail saying 'Cut my subscription,' telling us that they have ended the money they have been covenanting to give to us. Many Christian charities and agencies are in fact being determined in what they can say in their public and prophetic utterances by the bank. That's how far the old order is within the new.

How about the conventions and the culture around us? How about the attitude of the disciple group and of Jesus Himself? Jesus broke convention after convention. Of course, it hurt people around. It's interesting, some of us noted the other day, that among all the things Jesus came to do in the bringing of shalom, He has this enigmatic statement: 'I come not to bring shalom, but a sword.' Jesus' way towards God's shalom will involve all manner of non-shalom as families find themselves broken up, as relationships of the old order are called in question: when a man or woman has to stand true to the new; when father and son are divided; mother and daughter are divided. This sadness the early church had to wrestle with; we don't wrestle with it but perhaps we ought to?

Then there are the things Jesus did. For example, it was taboo to touch lepers or to touch the dead. Jesus embraced them. He raised the dead. It was taboo to share a meal with the untouchables. Jesus ran parties for them. Perhaps that's another thing that we should be thinking about, the extent to which Jesus in His lifestyle, used eating and drinking. And how close do we come to people in table fellowship? And how starved are those of us who close our homes to hospitality. It was against all right convention to go into the home of a pagan. Jesus did it again and again.

It was against the law for Jesus, or anyone, to travel with

women. Jesus had them ministering to Him. It was unconventional, against the custom, that forgiveness would be given to anyone without the price of a sacrifice being made in the temple. Jesus forgave men and women freely and called the marketplace where they did their sacrifices a den of thieves! It was taboo to have contact with prostitutes, but Jesus did and brought love again and again to the lives of loveless women.

It was against everything Jewish to break the unwritten rule of apartheid and have anything to do with the Samaritan. Yet again and again we find Jesus in Samaria, talking with Samaritans and hearing them and, God forgive Him, using the Samaritan as the symbol of the one who was neighbour.

Jesus not political? The whole lifestyle and all the values of the new order that He embodied and that He was sharing were a total challenge to every investment of those who had their investment in the old order. He deepened people's understanding of God's will. We are to love our enemies. We are to move the extra mile with the one who would compel us to go one. To despise others is, in God's eyes, a killing of them. What is outwardly beautiful, the whited sepulchre - beautiful, kept fresh with limewash - is inside decay and rot.

The fruit and gifts of the Spirit
Yet we can see that the early Christian community was true to the witness of Jesus and living the lifestyle of Jesus together. There's a verse, Romans 8:6, 'To set the mind on the Spirit is life and shalom.' We need only look at the nature of the fruit of the Spirit, and at the gifts of the Spirit to find how it was possible for the early community in their togetherness to give embodiment to the reign of God.

Those of us who are struggling to be obedient to the commands of Jesus and true to His expectations of us, except through the power of the Holy Spirit, are involved in a futile exercise. It is by the Spirit of God, of whom we have sung so much in our few days together. I wonder how much the one of whom we sing is honoured in our lives? 'To set the mind on the Spirit is life and shalom.'

Now a quick race through the fruit of the Spirit; we can't jump that. The fruit of the Spirit, quite quickly:

Agape - love, that's the first of them. That longing for the well-being of another that pursues the person's well-being even when that person kicks you in the teeth. That's the nature of agape; the love of God that pursues the undeserving, even when they throw it back at Him. Agape is consistency in the pursuit of the well-being of others, that kind of love.

Chara - joy. We've noticed already that chara is the experience of well-being; joy. It's the kind of - oh, there's no other word for joy - those who tease at words like happiness are trying from the old order to bring something across that is not chara. I'll have to leave it there.

Eirene - shalom. Yes, it's there right amidst the fruit of the Spirit, shalom.

Makrothumia - that means bearing with people for a long time. It means - there's a Scots word, forbearance. Do you have it down here? Do you have forbearance? You have? Oh good! All right! Forbearance, I thought that was Scots, that's really what makrothumia means. Stickability - being prepared to be alongside and to stay alongside and to stick with - makrothumia.

Chrestotes - that comes from a verb meaning to be of use. Helpfulness. Preparedness to be of use to another. The kind of person who is available, approachable and prepared to be of service.

Agathosune. Ah, that's a difficult one. Let's stick with goodness. That which is agathos is that which is of first rate quality and agathosune is being a person of first rate quality. I don't quite know what that means - a good guy, a person that you'll like to have around.

Pistis - well, this is the word for trust, it's the word for fidelity, it's the word for loyalty, it's the word for integrity. You can have your pick or you can put them all together. Fidelity, loyalty, integrity, trust. Commitment.

Prautes - a difficult one. It is the word that is translated as meek in 'blessed are the meek'. It means unpretentious, not self-assertive, not pushing yourself forward, - not being pushy, that's all right, not being a pushing person.

The last one - enkrateia - literally means power within; it's usually translated self control and I think that's probably not too far out. But it means something like strength of character, having the inner dynamic that can cope with the situation as it arises.

This is the fruit of the Spirit, we've not begun to look at the gifts and we're not going to have time to look at the gifts. Sufficient to say that, depending on how you count them, the actual listed gifts are either seventeen, nineteen or twenty-four. There's no statement made at any point that the gifts of the Spirit as listed are exhaustive. There may be any number more and it's quite fascinating to realise that in Romans 6:23, the charisma of God is eternal life. Perhaps the primary charismatic gift is eternal

life; the gift that comes from God's charis, God's longing and
searching for our well-being.

Fullness in the Spirit

Fullness of the Spirit. I'm conscious that we've had a group exploring
this during the day, so I don't need to say a great deal about
it, other than to have us see clearly that an alternative new order
lifestyle is impossible apart from the fullness of God's Spirit. Turning
the world upside down in the first few years of the Christian
community happened because of the fullness of the Spirit.

The nature of the fullness - well, perhaps it can be seen by
some of the parallels that we've got. We have fullness of the
Holy Spirit parallelled with fullness of wisdom, fullness of trust,
fullness of joy. We find it contrasted with fullness of deception,
fullness of fraud.

The person who is filled with joy is a person who is given
over to joy, a person who has no room for what is not joy, a
person who feels and expresses and radiates joy. And the joy of
such a person affects others. So the person who is filled with
the Holy Spirit feels, expresses and radiates Him. The person filled
with the Spirit is given over to Him, the person filled with the
Spirit has no room for that which is not of Him, and the Spirit-
filled person draws others to Christ. That's always been the ministry
of the Spirit.

It's important to see that being filled with the Spirit is not
some new idea, it's thoroughly biblical. It goes right back into
the Old Testament. It was experienced by John the Baptist; we're
told that he would be filled with Holy Spirit as soon as he was
born. It was experienced by his mother, who was filled full of
Holy Spirit. Jesus returned from the Jordan filled full of Holy Spirit.

And at Pentecost, the initial company of disciples were filled
full of Holy Spirit. You'll find that story in Acts 2. Later, Peter
again received this experience (Acts 4:8) and, having been filled
full of Holy Spirit, spoke with courage. Yet again during prayer
he and others (Acts 4:31) were filled full of Holy Spirit. Notice
the 'again' and 'again' and 'again'. Baptism in the Spirit may
be once for all; the fullness of the Holy Spirit is constantly to
be experienced. Paul expressly urges in Ephesians 5:18 that we
be continually filled full in Spirit.

In the Book of Acts there are 10 references to fullness of the
Spirit. The rest of the references are: 'seven accredited men, full
of Spirit and of wisdom'; 'Stephen, a man full of trust and the
Holy Spirit'; 'Barnabas, full of the Holy Spirit and of trust'; 'the

disciples at Antioch, continually filled full of joy and of Holy Spirit.'
Paul at his conversion and again later is 'filled full of Holy Spirit',
while Elimas the sorcerer is 'full of deception and fraud'.

Perhaps, finally on this bit, a look more closely at Paul's word
to the Ephesians: 'Together be continually filled full in the Spirit'
(Ephesians 5:18). Those to whom he was writing had already received
baptism in the Spirit and been sealed in the Spirit (Ephesians 1:13),
so the fullness of the Spirit was a different experience from that.

Then the verb is in the present tense which normally means
in Greek something that is a continuing happening, so it becomes
'be continually being filled' or 'go on being filled' or perhaps
'be filled again and again'.

Notice it's in the passive voice, the filling full of the Holy
Spirit is something to which we may be wholeheartedly open, but
it's not something we do for ourselves. 'Let Christ be filling you
full of Holy Spirit'. This is another expression of God's undeserved
love and all He's asking of us is the willingness to receive the
fullness of His Spirit. Notice it's plural in number and I suggest
that it is probably again one of those plurals that's addressed to
the community in their togetherness. It affirms our corporateness
in Christ, we are His community and He calls us to respond in
togetherness and know a communal filling in the Spirit. It's interesting
how groups of people together were filled in the Spirit; fullness
of Spirit puts an end to isolationism and individualism.

And then note, it's in the imperative mood - that means it's
a command. That means it's a command of the Lord, not an option
for the disciples. It's not for an elite among us, whatever we or
they might think. It's a demand of God that we be filled now.

Go into shalom
I'm going to stop there, I think, with just a few verses taken
at random, but I'm not going to get a chance to share with you,
about shalom, and I think you're beautiful. Jesus, as He speaks
with the disciples towards the end of His ministry, says, 'Shalom
I leave with you, my shalom I give to you.' And He speaks to
them again, 'that in me you might have shalom.' Romans 5:1,
'by faith we have shalom with God'; 2 Corinthians 13:11, 'live
in shalom with one another'; Ephesians 4:3, 'maintain the unity
of the Spirit in the bond of shalom'; Hebrews 12:14, 'follow shalom
with all men and holiness'; James 3:18, 'the fruit of justice is
sown in shalom by those who are making shalom'. That one's
not usually underlined. Romans 14:17, 'the kingdom of God is
justice, shalom and joy in the Spirit'. And just a few blessings

from Jude: 'mercy to you and shalom and love'. From any number of the letters, 'grace to you and shalom from God our Father and the Lord Jesus Messiah'. 2 Thessalonians 3:16, 'the Lord of shalom give you shalom'; Hebrews 13:20, 'may the God of shalom put you all to rights in everything good so that you can do His will'; Philippians 4:7, 'the shalom of God which passes all understanding keep your hearts and minds in the knowledge and love of God.'

The Lord bless you and keep you. The Lord make His face to shine upon you and be gracious to you. The Lord lift up the light of His countenance upon you and give you shalom.

Let's pray.

The Messianic Task

The reign of shalom

Some words from God's word. First a reading from Jeremiah, chapter 22, and then a few verses from 1 Peter, chapter 2. (reads Jeremiah 22:13). Not comfortable words. Thanks be to God for His word, even when it hurts, because God's hurt leads us to God's healing.

A quick recap on last evening. We looked together at the nature of the Gospel - the Good News - as Jesus brought it to us. God's good news. Good news of the Messiah, of Jesus, of the reign of God. Good news of God's inbreaking into our history in the person of Jesus to recreate His broken creation, to build in Jesus and through Jesus the new humanity. Jesus, the one anointed by the Spirit and with power, who went about doing good, anointed the Messiah, God's anointed one.

In Hebrews 7:2 Jesus is called the King of Shalom, taking up the prophecy of Isaiah - 'unto us a child is born, his name shall be the Prince of Shalom.' And in the King of Shalom there was present among us the kingdom or kingship or reign of God. And the signs that He performed as the King were evidence of God's reign among us. Jesus brought to men and women and to youngsters an experience of God's wholeness, as He reached out in love and recreated broken, twisted, thwarted, messed up lives.

That shalom, we discovered, meant more than peace, it meant wholeness, a total well-being, all that God's heart longs for His creation. A shalom, which, our hope, our certainty assures us, will come in Jesus, when the whole universe will bow down and acknowledge Jesus as Lord, to the glory of the Father. The longing of God is to bring shalom to the whole of creation and God's plan is to do this in Jesus.

Shalom not merely to the created world but to the world as

we experience it, to the world of our relationships, to our own selves as individual persons for whom God wants wholeness and healing in every part and longs to see us as integrated men and women, balanced, totally complete. People complete in body, complete in mind and heart and relationships, and with that openness to God and to His Spirit which enables us the only true freedom as a child before the father.

Shalom and salvation

We saw that this shalom was simply another way of describing God's salvation, His liberation in every area of our lives, from anything which thwarts or distorts shalom and into freedom and wholeness. This salvation comes to us because the only shalom man, Jesus, Himself went to the cross and taking Himself there as our representative suffered and died and shed His blood that we might experience God's wholeness, God's forgiveness, God's Fatherhood and be brought into His people as members of the new family and the new humanity.

We saw that shalom and salvation are always a gift from God and not of our achieving or our deserving. A gift that we receive as we open our lives in simple trust to the recreating Spirit of Almighty God. And we saw that openness in God's heart, that longing for our wholeness, is God's grace and we looked at the nature of grace as God's longing for our total well-being. And it was in the heart of God that our wholeness begins, in the heart of God our wholeness continues and in the heart of God that our wholeness will be complete.

In the death of the Messiah there was a new covenant made between humankind and God. And Jesus, as He sat at the Last Supper, as He broke the bread and handed out the wine, spoke of the new covenant in His blood, the promised covenant that the prophets had spoken of, the new covenant of shalom.

And on the day of Pentecost, when God's Spirit was poured out and a people was messiahed, we had the creation under God of the Messianic people of God, the people empowered and enabled by God's Spirit to be God's new humanity, moving towards God's new creation. And so we were born, God's family, by the power of God's Spirit, a new covenant people, a shalom people, a messianic people and we were called upon and created to give expression now to the kingdom.

This kingdom will come in its fullness when Jesus returns, but we are now called upon, enabled by God's Spirit, His power, His love, His gifts to give embodiment and expression to the reign

of God in the midst of an unredeemed world. We are called to
be the avante garde of the new creation, (first fruits is the Authorised
Version's translation). The avante-garde of the new creation we
are called upon to be and enabled to be, and so we move tonight
to looking at the nature of the task before the messianic people.

King, prophet and priest

Looking back into the Old Testament, there were three groups
of persons who were messiahed - only three - the kings, the prophets
and the priests. (Our translation perhaps disguises the fact that
lots of people were messiahed and there were also objects that
were sacred to God within the tabernacle that were messiahed.)
They were anointed as representing both the people and God, as
standing in a unique relationship between God and the world -
three persons: the king, the prophet and the priest.

The little kings were asked to reign after the manner and within
the confines that would be true of the big king when he came.
All the kings of Israel were required to carry through their kingship
as the big king would do when he came. So none of the kings
of Israel was free to do as he liked, to treat the people as he
chose and every one of the kings was under the voice of the
prophets, because the prophet could call the king back to being
true to his messianic role.

The little prophets - and there were false prophets - were called
upon to conduct their prophethood in the light of the big prophet
when he came. And the little priests to conduct their priesthood
in the light of the big priest when he came.

Prophets, priests and kings were not muddled up and did not
take up one another's function, because the one who came would
in himself be the one who would be the king and the prophet
and the priest. Until that time God's people would have all three
little ones, king, prophet and priest.

And then came Jesus, the Messiah, God's anointed one, anointed
in God's Spirit, and He came as The Prophet, as The Priest and
as The King. He came to bring among us the very nature of
God's kingship, to embody and demonstrate and share the reign
of God. He came as prophet to be God's representative before
the world, standing before us as the one in whom we saw God,
as the one who spoke for God, as the one who lived for God,
as the one who acted for God. He came as God's representative
to the cosmos. Turning that around, He also came as the priest,
the one who represented the cosmos before God. He appeared before
God as one of us, speaks as one of us, acts as one of us, lives

as one of us, as our representative before God.

So the Messiah comes as the one who is Himself bringing God's reign among us, as God's prophet, representing God to the cosmos, as the representative of the cosmos before God. This is the nature of His Messiahship.

A royal people

We could spend longer talking about the Messiahship of Jesus but we're talking tonight about the Messianic people, because if we belong to God through Jesus Christ and I'm not yet able to dispense with that little word 'if'. I'm conscious tonight that there may be friends, loved friends who are still outside of the family of God and I pause to challenge those of you who know someone with us tonight as a friend to be in prayer.

Unashamedly I say to anyone here who is not yet a brother or sister in Jesus, I covet you as a brother or a sister. I long for you to come into our family and my longing is nothing close to the longing in God's heart.

But if we are in God, through trust in Jesus Christ, we have been messiahed and we've been caught up with Jesus and we are given a job to do and this is it: to be a kingly people; to be a prophetic people; to be a priestly people. All I'm asking us to do tonight is to look a little more closely at what it means to be a shalom people caught up with the Messiah as He brings God's cosmos back to God.

Let's notice that the old Israel was baptised into Moses. Let's notice that the new Israel, God's new humanity, is baptised into Christ, baptised into the Messiah, baptised - there is one baptism - baptism in the Spirit of God and we are baptised in one Spirit into one Body.

The royal people. What does it mean to be a royal, kingly people? First of all and obviously it means that we are a royal family - WE ARE A ROYAL FAMILY - we have become children of the king. We have access not to the servants' quarters, not to the quarters of the administrations or the secretariats, we have access directly to the innermost chamber of the Father. If that hasn't been obvious tonight, I don't know what has. We need none save Jesus as our entry to the Father. It's an incredible thought if our minds could contain it, that we actually are children of God, with all the privileges of God's children.

The apostles dared to say that we reign with Him! What of our long faces, what of our lack of power, our dejection, our lack of hope, our lack of enthusiasm? What of our apprehensions and our scarednesses - and, yes, He is aware of all of these - because we are not aware of what it is to be His sons and daughters? We may be glad that God is king and that as His sons and daughters we have one who understands us utterly, but there is no need for the fearfulness, the fretting, the apprehensions, the lack of hope and the lack of joy. There is no need of us being cowed by the world, because we are children of God. And I long, as I guess so many of us do, that our lives may be brought to the kind of buoyancy under God in which we are free to be what we are.

A new nation

But let's notice this one too (and it was quite clear in our reading from Peter) that the day we place our trust in Jesus the Messiah, there is a transfer of nationality. To be a member of the kingdom, to be a kingly people involves a transfer of nationality.

It took me a long time to understand, because all Scots are nationalists. I have on several occasions - I don't know how it will count in glory - found myself voting Scottish Nationalist and if you understood Scottish heritage you might understand that. But I understand now, that in Jesus Christ, that all forms of nationalism are part of the old order. In Jesus Christ we belong to a new nation. I'm not a Scottish nationalist, I'm not free to be a British nationalist - that's the option we're usually given - I'm not free to be any other kind of nationalist than one of the kingdom of the Messiah.

The Christian community, then, is not an international community; we are a new nation and our place in the other nations of the world is as aliens. Did you notice what Peter called us - aliens and exiles? We no longer belong in the nations of the old order, except as aliens called upon under God to live responsibly in the countries which give us the right to be there.

We have no rights, we belong to the new order, we belong to a new nation. Paul tells us quite clearly in Philippians - he tells us the politeuma - that our politeuma - our government, the place where decisions are made affecting the new nation is with God. Our politeuma is not with this Caesar, or that Caesar, or this Czar, or that Czar, or this King, Queen or President or governor. Our politeuma is with God.

That's not how we've lived since Constantine and some of us are going to do a lot of thinking. What does it mean that in trusting Jesus our nationality is transferred to the new nation?

But I must explain this a bit more. I'm sorry if we keep throwing new things or throwing old things into new patterns. Today I tried to describe to someone how God has given us truth and truths which all direct us towards truth. And its rather as if we had those truths in a children's kaleidoscope and some of us never move the kaleidoscope and we get accustomed to a particular pattern into which the pieces fit and we can get really comfortable with this pattern.

Then someone comes along and gives it the gentlest little twist. Nothing's happened to the contents, they're just thrown into a new juxtaposition with each other and I suggest to you that one of the most creative things we can do is to allow God's word to come freshly into new relationships, so that things we've begun to believe we can contain and can hold and pocket, can challenge us anew.

What we have done since the time of Constantine is to decide: 'No, God, we don't want to be a new nation. That's really tough. Right up into the time of Constantine we tried that and it was really tough.' They had to live in caves, they didn't have so much as a church building. The group that turned the world upside down never had a building to work in. They had no committees nor any of the resources available to us, because they were a banned people and the reason for that was that they were being, under God, a new nation.

Now a nation has at the very heart of it - can I use the word cultus and be understood? No? A cultus is the word that describes what happens round an altar or a communion table when people come in order to do specifically religious things around a specifically religious focus. OK, that's the cultus. Now a nation has a cultus at the centre of it. The temple was the centre of the old Israel. Now God asks us to be a new nation but what we decided was: 'No, thank you very much, God, we don't want to be a new nation. What we will do, though, is become the cultus at the centre of the old nation. We don't want to be a new order nation, let's just be the bit round the altar in one of the old nations.'

So we made a little deal with the Roman empire, and the bishops and the Emperor shook hands. The result was the bishops all became civil servants operating the Roman empire and the church retreated into the bits that were supposed to be religious, and the redemption of God's creation was left to go hang. And God's people were no longer concerned with being a nation, living the life of a new order with its new values and everything else. 'No thank you, Lord. We find it much easier to spend our time round the altar, singing hymns, saying prayers.'

And out there we obey Caesar and we've got caught up in something very foolish, and, of course, we're not persecuted for it; we're not persecuted for that at all, because it's doing no damage to the demonic at all. There's nothing for the principalities and powers to fear if they've got us chained in as chaplains, giving some kind of official respectability to the old order.

But we are a kingly people living in the midst of the old order as a new nation, aliens everywhere else but called upon to be responsible and caring aliens. However, we don't live that way and are continually finding ourselves compromised, supporting oppression and injustice in the name of God.

For example, isn't it a blasphemy that God, who in Jesus is undoing the effects of the Fall, can't expect among His own people to find a new understanding of womanhood as we see it in the life and discipling of Jesus. I'm happy to feel that in the communities that are open to God's Spirit something quite new and different is happening.

Making things anew

We are to be the avante-garde of the new creation. Maybe I can throw in one or two new things about that. Another of the things that we got at the time of Constantine, apart from our nonsense in losing our nationhood, was that we started to talk in a number of divides.

One of them was that we started to talk of the divide between the material and the spiritual. This is not a biblical divide, it is not a kingdom divide. The Bible doesn't divide life into the material and the spiritual - the Bible divides life into the old order and the new order.

And the new order has materiality about it. We have bodies - God graced our bodies in Jesus. We have bodies, we have physicality, we have sexuality - praise God for them! These aren't negatives. These are part of God's creation and recreation, and the new peoplehood of the new order must glory in the material as it is lived under the Spirit of God. The opposite of spiritual is non-spiritual and the opposite of material is non-material. But in the new order we take up the totality of the material, of the physical, of our bodies, of our relationships, which, as they are opened to the Spirit of God, become a means of expressing the nature of God's new creation.

What other means does God have than that which He has lovingly made and lovingly is remaking? Let's not despise the body, let's not despise material things. They are of God's making and God's loving. Let's bring God's creation and open it and place it again under the responsibility of His Spirit, and in that way, evidence before the world the kind of things that turn the world upside down.

Let's recognise that we brought in a divide between soul and body. That's not a biblical divide. The word nephesh which we translate soul in the Old Testament, is the word for the complete being, the totality of a person. Body, soul and spirit are ways of seeing the totality in different ways; they are not different parts that are lopped off and divided. So God sees us as complete persons, as complete beings.

Perhaps - I would suggest to you - I haven't pursued this one with the thoroughness with which I can stand with full conviction behind it, so I'm giving you a little thing that I'm currently chasing along. Anyway, I believe that when the contrast comes between spirit and flesh that we are actually talking about spirit as the order of the new community of God's Spirit, as opposed to the old order, which was flesh.

And I find the wrestling between spirit and flesh is a wrestling between that which is in the new order of God's spirit and that which is still caught up in the old order. There seems to me to be a conflict: that a whole big part of me is comfortable and happy in the old order and wants to embrace the demonic and be available to it, but God's urgings and God's longings carry me across into the new. Until Christ comes we are caught up in this conflict between the old order and the new.

Maybe a last thing - Ephesians 3:10 - Paul's longing that through the church, the ecclesia, the multi-coloured (I like that word, it comes again and again) wisdom of God should be declared to the principalities and powers. That means that the principalities and powers of evil should have cause to tremble because of the existence of God's people.

A prophetic people

Quickly on to the prophetic. If we are to be God's prophetic people, what does that mean? Well, it means first of all that we've got to be God's representatives wherever He has placed us. We have got to be present in the world, not abstracted from it and living at the edge of it, but actually penetrating the world. The church for far too long has been absent from the places where life is dirty and where life hurts. And if we are to be truly a messianic and prophetic people we must be at the places where life is painful, where difficult, complex decisions are being made and especially at those places where the demonic is claiming control of God's world.

The salt of the earth

One illustration that I've found very helpful for this (and I thank David Pawson for correcting some of my understanding of the words of Jesus) is when Jesus calls us the salt of the earth. It's Matt. 5:13 I'm referring to. I assumed always that this meant that we were there as a preservative or perhaps to give a little bit of flavour, because I like salt as a flavouring and I know in some parts of the world salt acts much the way that curry does and gives a kind of preservative to meat that's rotting. But David Pawson says it doesn't mean that at all.

Here's what Jesus says: 'If the salt has lost its saltiness, it is no longer, no longer fit for the soil or for the dung hill, but is thrown aside and trodden underfoot by men.' Now that 'no longer' is important; it's lost its saltiness and is no longer fit for the soil or the dunghill. What does that mean?

Well, as it turns out there are parts of the world where salt is scattered lightly across soil that has got compacted together and the salt breaks it up and allows the moisture to go down and allows things to grow up. The salt is actually a fertiliser enabling new life and Jesus was drawing on that agricultural picture to show that His disciples were to be a fertiliser in the world.

But rather more boldly, the second part of Jesus' saying. At the bottom of the yard - as still happens in some places, even in some luxurious places you might go on holiday in France and some other places - you've got a little privy at the bottom of the garden, which actually turns out to be a pit. And in the time of Jesus, at the side of that pit polite houses would provide a large mound of salt. Yes, you've got it! Guests covered the waste with salt which acted as a sealant against nasty smells and as a disinfectant against disease.

So, Jesus was telling His disciples, with a smile no doubt (and much of Jesus' teaching has got smiles in it, and we read it with such deadly seriousness!), but behind the smile there is point that he means His people to be up against the crap in the world. Tight up against it, protecting others from its rottenness and its decay. And if God's people will sit in little heaps refusing to have anything to do with the crap in the world, we are refusing to be the salt of the earth. That metaphor is not mine and if you find it uncomfortable, so do I.

God asks us as His people to permeate the old order and to

be there in Jesus to bring life and to bring healing. From the passage that we read from Ezekiel we could see that God says, 'This is to know me - to do justice.' Some of us are already a little concerned at this particular emphasis that we're finding in God's word, that to know God is to do justice.

In John's first letter he says that those who do not love do not know God. He doesn't say that when you know God the consequence will be that you will do justice. One is not the cause and the other the effect, they go together. Knowing God involves doing justice and the person who claims to love God and does not love other people is deceived and is not loving God when they do not love other people.

And we're called upon to be a prophetic people and to stand as Jesus stood over a city and weep; as He stood looking at the city, He wept. And the prophets loved the people, the villages, the towns to which God sent them with the consequences of their lives.

Justice in the city

I think that it is clear that we are called upon in Jesus to be involved as a community of His people, as various communities of His people, in healing, in bringing wholeness. We are called upon to bring justice, to stand alongside the little people, the homeless people, the poor people, the folk whose lives and families are all broken up and fragmented. The people whose lives are caught up with one drug or another. The people whose lives are without hope. We are called upon to identify with and speak up for them.

Maybe a last thought or two about Jesus in the Beatitudes. Ask yourself what difference it makes. Does Jesus say 'blessed are those who hunger and thirst after righteousness' (that's the Authorised Version)? Does it make a difference that that word translated righteousness is the ordinary Greek word for justice? 'Blessed are those who hunger and thirst for justice'? Does that make a difference? I believe it does. In being a man or woman of justice, we must be men and women of righteousness. We've got by for too long with moving towards a righteousness which has got nothing to do with justice.

Let's look at Jeremiah 29:7. God's people had been carried into captivity, into the city of Babylon, and of all the places where they did not want to be, the most hated was Babylon. It represented in Jewish history everything that was opposed to God, the very centre of idolatry itself, and God allowed His people to be placed in captivity in Babylon. Do you feel, living in 1978, that God's

people are again in Babylon? There are a great many signs that
that's what's happened.

Now hear the word that God gave to Jeremiah to speak to
God's people in Babylon: 'Seek the shalom of the city where I
have sent you and pray to the Lord on its behalf, for in its shalom
you will find your own shalom.'

I wanted to say a few words on the nature of making disciples.
Can I take it as read that part of the prophetic ministry is sharing
the Good News of Jesus Christ, of sharing the Good News of
His death, His resurrection, His Spirit, sharing the Good News
of the new peoplehood and calling men and women and young
people into discipleship. That is central to the prophetic message.

A priestly people

Our last message, the priestly one. Again it requires, if we are
going to represent the people, a penetration and an identification.
The priesthood of all believers is something that probably many
people in this room treasure. It was an understanding that we
came back to from God's word at the Reformation, that humanity
needs none between itself and God save Jesus.

But what does the priesthood mean? If we are a priesthood,
those of us who belong to Jesus, on whose behalf are we priests?
A priest is someone who links another to God, who stands as
a go-between. Are you a priest on your own behalf? No, you're
not. Jesus is your priest. Are you a priest on my behalf? No,
you're not. Jesus is my priest. And we together are caught up
as priests in Him. Then on whose behalf are we a priesthood?

We can only be a priesthood on behalf of those who are not
priests, therefore the astonishing thing that comes to light is that
God's people are called to be a priesthood on behalf of those
who are outside of Christ. And if we spend all our time in our
togetherness as a little priestly huddle, chanting and singing hymns
to one another, we are not being a priesthood, because a priesthood
acts in a representative capacity on behalf of those who are not
priests. And if we are not alongside of them, sharing their agonies,
how do we bring them to God? If we don't know their hurts,
how do we offer their hurts to God? If we don't know the things
they're struggling to find words of praise to utter how can we
utter them on their behalf.

And to become a priesthood, means to get alongside the little
people, the hurting people, and the big people, because the oppressors
are as much oppressed by their oppressing as those they are oppressing.
To be a priesthood on behalf of the world and indeed on behalf

of creation, we must be alongside, agonising with it at the points
of its need and its hurt and identifying with that hurt as Jesus
did. We must be those moved by God's Spirit whose weeping
is a real weeping, whose hurting is a real hurt and we'll come
to understand once again what it means to suffer.

It's very, very easy for Christians to make pronouncements about
moral things where they have had nobody in their family and
none of their friends going through the trauma of hurt that other
people are going through. As soon as you get alongside someone
who is hurting, who really is caught up in moral struggle, you
cease to speak with the confidence of condemnation and you weep
and agonise alongside. And you come before God pleading.

And the place of God's people as a priesthood must be one
of suffering. Not suffering on our own behalf, not suffering for
the things we do - suffering alongside of others, and because of
others and because of their need and their hurt and because they
are suffering in the heart of our Father.

We must intercede on behalf of the world that's broken, a world
that's lost. We can hardly pick up a newspaper, we can hardly
listen to a newscaster, but we find we've shut out the horror of
a broken world. Alone we cannot be priests; together under God
by His Spirit we can. And intercession is a responsibility He has
placed upon us. Alongside of that agonising and that suffering
and sharing in the world's need, praise God, there is praise and
priests come to praise, to laugh, to joy, priests come to celebrate,
priests come to dance.

And one of the things God asks us to be as His priestly community
is a group of men and women and young people who are showing
the world what the reality of hope is, what the rediscovery of
life and beauty and wholeness is about. And that's one of the
functions of the priesthood.

A living sacrifice

I'd like to catch all of that up under worship. It's very hard in
the Bible to find a word that means what we call worship. The
Bible words all refer to the things that we do in every little part
of our lives. Even in Romans 12:1, the translators cannot decide
whether to translate that by worship or by service, because it's
the same Greek word for both. 'Present your body as a living
sacrifice, which is your reasonable worship? ...service?' Wouldn't
it be wonderful if we allowed the Holy Spirit to bring us to the
point where there was no division between our worship and our

service, because what we were doing in the world was so honouring to God that it was worship and where our worship is of the nature that the world coming in fell down on its face and said, 'Surely God is among you.' I believe that when our lives are open in this gathering and we're really worshipping God, someone coming in knows God is here. I will pray that for our churches.

Finally, the kind of kingship, the kind of prophethood, the kind of priesthood that Jesus demonstrated was always as a servant. He didn't come as the king who lorded it over us, He came as the king who served, as the prophet who served, as the priest who served, even to death. And God's people must be people of servanthood, people whose attitudes and values are not those of the old order. It may be that we will find ourselves in our hearts having to ask God for forgiveness and asking for new values that come of His Spirit.

The Messiah was crucified and the Messianic people must look to being crucified if it's being true to Jesus. To take up our cross daily does not mean simply to run the risk of someone shouting 'yah boo' or something behind us. To take up our cross daily means to commit ourselves to the social ostracism, to the antagonism of the old order and to what the old order has done every time the new order has been true to itself. That means suffering, it means crucifixion.

When Jesus called upon His disciples to take up their cross daily, He was asking them to take upon themselves the symbol of death and to move with him as representatives of God's reign towards the new creation. The Messiah was the Messiah because He was anointed by the Spirit. The Messianic people is the Messianic people because it is anointed by the Holy Spirit.

I have two questions to ask us tonight. Can we take up our cross? Have we been to the cross? It's the only place where we meet the Messiah. It's the only place where we join the kingdom. Have you been to His cross? Have you found your life's gained its only significance as you knelt there? Have you paused at any moment in life to understand the nature of the death of Jesus for you? And do you know the anointing of the Holy Spirit? Do you know what it is to be one whose life is indwelt by God's Spirit? Have you been to the cross? Have you entered into Pentecost?

Let's pray.

Announcing the Messiah

Introducing Luke

Last time we got together on Luke we had a very quick look at what makes Luke different. Each of the New Testament writers is different and clearly comes from a different background. God brought them up in different ways with different circumstances, so truth, as it comes to us from different people, comes to us differently. Different things excite them, different things emphasise what God has given them. That doesn't mean they are saying different things, but that God gave the truth to them in different ways, with different perceptions.

Luke is one of the exciting characters in the New Testament. We recognised that he was a physician, most of whom were slaves in the first century and that his name is a diminutive. Luke probably was a freed slave. The chances are that he came from Macedonia; he may even have been the man from Macedonia of Paul's dream, in Acts 16:9. He certainly spent quite a bit of time in Philippi. He's mentioned by Eusebius, in his anti-Marcionite prologue, as being a Syrian from Antioch. If that's the case, then he was obviously taken from there, or his father was taken from there, probably as a slave, and later became a free man. Some have suggested that he was actually set free by a guy called Theophilus. If that is true then it would be fascinating, because, of course, he addresses his gospel to Theophilus and if Theophilus had been the man who had set him free and had become a Christian then that would be very exciting.

We certainly know that he had intimate contact with very key people in the missionary enterprise. We know that from the time he joined Paul he became his devoted friend and stuck with him through the last few years of his life. And, as far as we know, though Acts finishes before the death of Paul, Luke would have been with Paul at the very end. It may be that Paul's health necessitated him having somebody with him who was a physician. There is some hint that, in terms of the flesh, Paul wasn't allowed to be an apostle who was completely well and it may be that he needed a constant physician. But whatever, Luke was obviously a devoted friend to Paul.

At the beginning of the gospel you can see how carefully Luke tried to get contact with his sources. And he is actually a very careful historian. Several people down the years have tried again and again to burst the balloon that has been Luke, to try and find him to be unreliable and they haven't managed that. There are still a couple of things hanging around that haven't quite been put right, but at place after place evidence has come up and Luke has been found to be in possession of the actual knowledge, for which, until supporting evidence came up, we were totally reliant on Luke. So he has actually been proved to be very reliable historian of the period.

The one area which is still doubtful, and it's not terribly important, is placing the taxation at the very beginning of the gospel (Luke 2:1), where he says: 'when Quirinius was governor.' In fact, as far as we know, the taxation took place several years later when Quirinius was indeed governor. We don't know who was governor at the early period. But, apart from that one instance, all the queries have fallen away and Luke has been found to be accurate; and there are scholars who maintain that Quirinius was in fact responsible for a census on two occasions. It's an interesting one that's still open. But Luke was a good historian.

It's quite obvious that Luke had a classical education. A lot of the slaves were infinitely better educated than their masters; in fact, very frequently the slaves were responsible for the education of the children. And it's quite clear that he had a very able mind: he writes the best Greek in the New Testament and yet he had the ability, that only a creative mind has, when he's turning to the passages of the Old Testament, suddenly to lapse into language which is not his own. In other words, he is able to make passages sound Olde Worlde and Semitic when writing in situations which require it. So he's a very skilled writer and he's been recognised as that by those who know the language well enough to identify that. He's been recognised as a man of a good mind.

Luke's gospel

I suggested before that he spent all the time in Caesarea with

Paul and that it was during the two or three years when he was free, while Paul was in prison, that he had the time to go up and down Palestine and make whatever contacts he could to verify the information he was trying to get. About fifty per cent of Luke's gospel is actually original, so, if we lost Luke we'd have lost a phenomenal amount that we wouldn't get from Matthew or Mark or John. And it's quite interesting, when we look at that original material, to see what material he brought together. We find one or two key notes of the things that obviously show something about the kind of guy Luke was, the kind of experience that he had.

We saw, for example, that his is the gospel of women. He is the guy who remarks again and again about women in a world where women were ignored by a people who were a lot more Jewish than he, and who had not quite so liberated an understanding as Luke of the significance and the importance of women. And particularly he shows us the place that women had in the life of Jesus. It seems likely that even the story in John's gospel about the woman taken in adultery was actually penned by Luke. You know in some of the versions it's actually relegated to a footnote. And that's not because it's not known to be original: it's because we don't know whether it belongs in Luke's gospel or in John's. A lot of the manuscripts have it in Luke and the language of that passage has got words that are unique to Luke and don't appear in John. In all probability then it's yet another story written by Luke about a woman and about Jesus' relationship to a woman.

We saw how particularly concerned Luke was for the poor and the oppressed and that he was the one who tells us quite clearly how Jesus Himself stood in solidarity with the powerless people, the little people, the oppressed people, the people who were otherwise insignificant. Luke was the one who particularly tells us that - it may be because his background attracted him to that in Jesus.

And Luke is the one who emphasises, from the beginning to end of the gospel, the places where Jesus seems to say something about the. gospel of the kingdom being for all people, a light to the Gentiles. He's the one who starts his gospel off with John the Baptist coming for all people, and then recording the words that came from Anna and Simeon in the temple. Talking about the Gentiles, Luke writes his gospel on the understanding that the good news that Jesus came was intended from the outset for the whole world. So there's that terrific vision that Luke gives us that we could have missed out on if we didn't have the emphasis that God gave us through Luke.

We should also recognise the extent to which Luke is the one who records the significance of prayer in the life of Jesus. Luke shows us again and again and again how, right in the midst of all His involvement, Jesus was one who turned to the Father. At every major place in His life we find Jesus in prayer before the decisions.

Furthermore, I don't think I emphasised enough last time how much Luke is the one who emphasises praise and song. Luke can quite rightly be said to be the first Christian hymn writer, the one certainly who first records for us the early Christian songs. If you look at the very beginnings of the gospel, you'll find that song after song after song that have moved down through the Christian tradition, like the Magnificat, like the Nunc Dimitus, like the Gloria in Excelsis, all come from Luke. They were known already but because he was a different guy from Matthew, a different guy from John, these things grabbed him. He liked singing and he obviously liked songs. The word 'joy' comes again and again and again in Luke; he was obviously a man of praise and a guy who loved to get caught up in celebration. And we recognised that he was a man for whom miracles mattered a great deal.

I'm going to draw attention today to the word 'angel' that appears more in Luke than in anybody else. So, although he's the guy who's most rooted in the practical, who sees the socio-political dimension of Jesus' life as none of the other writers do in quite the same way, at the same time, he is the guy who is most aware of the dimension of the eternal and of the transcendent breaking-in to the world of the material in a very powerful way. (Breaking-in, not to make a dichotomy, but to make possible the transformation of the life that we live.) And he's the one who makes the biggest emphasis on miracles. When we come to the Acts of the Apostles, we realise how supremely it is Luke who is conscious of the power of the Holy Spirit and if we hadn't the words of Luke and his record of the activities of the Holy Spirit, I think we would be a very much poorer community in our understanding of what God can do and of who God is.

So those were the kind of thoughts that we looked at last time. And we decided to zone in a little bit today on some of these ideas and try to take one or two lead thoughts from Luke. So what I'm going to do is a series of word studies, based on these verses in Luke 2, that's Luke 2: 8-11. Sometimes I think it would be liberating for us if we went back to the first century where people had to learn God's word because they hadn't copies of it for themselves and therefore listened really carefully when

it was read, and memorised it. And they had it read out again
and they repeated it one to the other. Today, because we've actually
got it between covers and we can say, 'Och well, I can look
at that,' well we drift away and the preciousness of this thing
doesn't always grab us, even if we've got the nicest little Bible
and we do mark it occasionally. I've the feeling that maybe if
we were back in the first century we might treasure God's word
when we heard it in a more powerful way.

'To the shepherds...'

But just now, we'll look at some simple words that we know
very, very well. Words that were said to a group of completely
undesirable men, men who epitomised what it was to be outcasts
and men to whom God gave an incredible message. I'm talking
about shepherds. We have the idea at Christmas time that shepherds
were somehow a nice pastoral group of people, everybody's friends,
coming down with the sheep to the villages. They were nothing
of the kind. The shepherds were despised, they were outcasts, and
did not function in the Temple. And so right there, God bringing
that particular message of His glory and His joy to a group of
the most outcast people within society, is quite important. That's
a strange thing in view of the extent to which God was even
called a shepherd in the Old Testament, but in the time of Jesus
the shepherds were outcasts. The only people who were worse were
the pig herders.

Interestingly, I found recently that the word that was used
by the Zealots, the Jewish resistance movement, for the Romans
- you won't believe this, well you might - the Romans were called
pigs. And that's astonishing when you read the story of Jesus,
when he went to the guy who was possessed by demons. The
name he was called by was a Roman name. I don't know what
you're going to make of this, but the Roman name, which only
existed in the Roman world, was a military word, 'Legion'. And
it was from 'Legion' that the demons were cast and they went
into the pigs. I have a sneaking feeling that behind that story
lies either a lot of humour or a very powerful prophetic message
to the people of that time. But that's not what we're on at the
moment, but that is in our Bible, and, if we know little bits of
what is there, suddenly a whole new light and new possibilities
can be shed on many passages.

'To the shepherds who were in the open country' - hardly
in fields despite most of our translations, they didn't have fields
- 'looking after their flocks. And an angel of the Lord stood near

to them and the glory of the Lord shone round about them and they feared a great fear. And the messenger said to them, "Fear not, for lo, I am evangelising to you a great joy, which shall be to all people. That which was born to you today is a saviour, who is the Messiah, the Lord."'

Let's look at the terms we've got. First of all I want to look at this 'evangelising', for that's what the word is, and I want to look at how Luke uses evangelism and evangelising. 'I bring you tidings of great joy' is the one we like to use at Christmas time, but the word is evangelising and if that is going to change your understanding of evangelism, then so be it. I'd like to look at 'joy'. I'd like to look at 'people' and then, if we've got time, at the actual message, 'A saviour, the Messiah, the Lord'. OK?

'...the messenger'

Just a quick thing on 'angel' that I've jotted down. 'Angel' is a difficult one for us today and I wish somebody would help me get to terms with it. I tried reading Billy Graham's book and I don't think that that got me in touch with what the New Testament is really trying to say. But in the absence of anybody else, I commend him for trying because it's a very difficult area.

It is interesting to note that when John the Baptist sent guys to speak to Jesus, Luke in 7:24 says, 'when the angels of John were departed.' The word angelos, from which we get the word angels, is the word for someone who is the bearer of a message. It's an ordinary word for one who was a courier; a despatch rider would have been called an angelos. And John sent people off as his representatives to Jesus to question what He was about and Luke reports, 'when the angels of John were departed.'

That gives a little hint, but it doesn't clear the difficulty, because again and again and again it's Luke who records messengers of God, using names for them that had been used by the Jews to refer to very major beings at the peak beyond God's creation of man. Luke uses the word angelos 47 times, Mark uses it 6, John uses it 4 and Matthew 21 times. This will give you some idea of how the concept of God as a communicator, as God dealing face to face with humanity, is really important to Luke. 47 times in Luke! That's all I'm going to say.

Goodnewsing

I want to start off with the euangelizesthai. The first time that Luke uses this word is in chapter 1, verse 19 and the words are coming from the mouth of Gabriel, who says to Zechariah, the old priest who was to be John the Baptist's father, 'I am sent to speak to you and to evangelise these things to you.' In other words, Gabriel has come with a gospel, with good news. I'm not sure what to do with this word because it doesn't read right to us to translate it that way, and yet if we don't then we're missing out on a lot of dimensions in Luke that help us to understand what the gospel actually was.

Although we call it good news, euangelion does not mean good news. We make those first two letters eu mean good, but they don't actually. They are actually the word for well; not an adjective good, but an adverb well. And eu angelion is actually something that is well announced. That means that it could be bad news, thoroughly or adequately or completely announced. And it is argued that euangelion is used for example of the news of the Fall. 'Publish it not in the streets of Ashpodel', in that passage, in the Greek translation, for that bad news, the word euangeleon is used.

So it may not be a word that actually means good news. And to some of us, the message that God brings, while it may bring goodness to us, and always will, if it's God's word for us, may in fact not be welcome and our idea that this is 'joyful tidings' may in fact miss out on the nature of the gospel. Sometimes the word gospel is used in the New Testament when people are being addressed in a very powerful and frightening way that will demand a major change in life. Later on it may be glad tidings, but when they heard it first, it certainly didn't waken a lot of joy. We have to be careful not to turn this into a soft word. It's a very powerful word and God's word of judgement can be 'gospel'.

There's too much of an old debate coming back in some circles that puts law and gospel into some kind of funny relationship, that says because we speak of God's call to obedience, we've suddenly moved out of grace. That's not a biblical way of thinking at all. God's word of judgement comes to us from God's grace. So, 'good-newsing' is as close as I can get to it, but I want to be careful about the 'good' bit so that I know what we are saying.

Goodnewsing repentance

'I am sent to speak to you and to goodnews these things to you, to announce these things to you.' And the kind of things that were said to Zechariah earlier and related to that gospel were that his prayer had been heard, that he was going to father a son; that many were going to rejoice because of John's existence and John would be full of the Spirit from his birth (that's a very difficult one); he will turn many to God and will come in the Spirit and the power of Elijah; turn fathers back to their children and prepare a people for the Lord. Now all of that was stunning: he was an evangelist.

The next time euangelion is used is in the passage we read and will return to, the word to the shepherds. It's next occurrence is in Luke 3:18. We're talking of John the Baptist now, we're told that he evangelised the people. Now perhaps you've not thought of him as an evangelist but he was, the same as Gabriel, he evangelised the people.

In verse 3 we find him heralding a baptism of metanoia, towards a release from failure. Now that's very literal and not very good English. He was heralding a dipping, if you like; the word baptism is used in secular Greek outside of the New Testament, to describe someone being overwhelmed by death or completely being taken over by alcohol. It's a word of overwhelming, of engulfing, of being swamped, of being completely given over to. Now some people have made it into inundation, and then into sprinkling or whatever, but those meanings don't lie in the word. The word itself was a word of dipping, submerging, not necessarily immersing, engulfing and swamping.

And John came with a message of metanoia. We usually translate that as repentance. Meta means change, noia is attitude, outlook. John came with a message that required our total orientation, our understanding, our outlook on life, to undergo a radical change, as our lives were open to the Spirit of God and as we entered into the new order that he was proclaiming, the order of the Messiah and turned away from the old order. That meant a release. The word for forgiveness in Greek is the ordinary word for release from failure.

And the Lord was coming, that was part of John's message, part of his gospel. In verse 6, 'all flesh shall see the salvation of God.' Here we've got Luke stating it quite clearly that God has no longer limited His purpose to the people of Israel. God has extended through the people of Israel; through this son who was born, God has extended His salvation to the world. 'The axe is laid at the root of the tree,' in other words, God is chopping trees down and the axe is right at the roots and they are going to topple. That's still part of the gospel - there are trees that God is about to chop.

Also still part of the gospel, are the fruits that are deserving of being called metanoia. These are the acts that give evidence of the radical turn around in attitude and understanding that is to happen when someone responds to the gospel. The person with two coats shares, the person with more fruit shares with those who have not fruit. This is part of the good news as proclaimed and those people who turned round and said, 'what about us?' were very practical. The soldiers said it, the tax collector said it. They posed big problems for him, but John was able to apply the message of the kingdom to the lives of the people who were living in the world.

He clearly told people not to exploit, and he told the soldiers to be content with their wages. We're too ready to assume that he meant people should always be happy with what they're given and that if we live in a society where we pay people a pittance to serve us, that's what God wants. That's not what He wants at all! What John was telling the soldiers was that they were not to supplement their income in the way that the Roman soldiers were free to do in first century Palestine, which was simply to take money when they wanted it. If they ran out of their weekly wages they simply extorted it. It happens still today in societies which are run in that way and where the military are allowed in an unjust way to get control. So John was telling them to be content with their wages: 'Make your wages do. Stop exploiting the people, don't repress, don't misrepresent, don't falsely accuse them.'

Goodnewsing the poor

Then the next time the word euangelion comes up it is on the lips of Jesus, when He stands up in the synagogue and says, 'The Spirit of the Lord is upon me because He has messiahed me to evangelise the poor.' In other words, Jesus has brought good news to the people and the poor of the earth. The word that's there for poor is the commonest word for poor in the New Testament and it means cringing, all doubled up. It means a person who has been brought to the point in relationship with other people that they always come kind of cowed. The poor are the people who have been made to count for nothing, who have got no sense of their own worth.

Now Matthew - where Jesus says 'blessed are the poor', adds another couple of words, and we've latched on to them to avoid the edge of what Jesus was saying. Luke quite clearly records the word of Jesus as 'blessed are the poor', Matthew puts it 'blessed are the poor in spirit' and so we've turned that round and we've cleverly managed to make it mean not the people who are poor, but the people who are spiritually needy. It does mean that, but it means that because it means people who have been so reduced as people that they are totally dis-spirited; they are poor at every level of life to the point that they have absolutely nothing to allow them to stand up with any value or respect or worth.

So the poor in spirit, far from allowing us to escape and say, 'Ah well, of course, what it really means is... ,' actually shows us the very nature of what we can do to people. It shows that we can so reduce other people, that far from standing up to be the free beings that God made us to be in an inter-related open freeness, they become totally dis-spirited and broken. So Jesus had come, He was messiahed, to evangelise the poor. He said that quite clearly.

Some of us are beginning in this community to experience Jesus' freedom, many of us for the first time, because we have our different ways of being reduced in spirit. It was the purpose of His being messiahed and I don't think God gave us these words to make us feel guilty, to make us bask in guilt that immobilises us, but that's actually what we allow to happen again and again.

We are all wealthy. I know the way you live and I feel very guilty sometimes when I am among you. Can I be honest about that? I know I shouldn't feel guilty and I ask forgiveness for that. But I do sometimes feel very guilty.

Last summer, for example, someone in the cottage where I was staying handed in a pair of shoes and when I saw how excited another person was at being handed a pair of boots, I almost wept. I've not lived in that, you see, and that really got right home to me and nobody did anything about it. The whole community was perfectly accepting, all rejoicing together because somebody handed in a pair of boots and I was almost immobilised. I almost couldn't speak. I don't understand it, but I think it's beautiful and the kind of thing we've got to experience before we find the freedom that will allow us to identify with the poor in the way that Jesus asks us to do.

There must be some reason why you are moving towards that kind of disassociation from personal possessions. Not that we don't still treasure things and that things don't have beauty and meaning for us, but we can be separated from them without grief. That enables us, as the early church found, to identify with the people who are the least, the littlest and the neediest. And Jesus came Himself in that position with a message of good news for the poor.

I'd recommend to some of you this book, 'The Englishman's Greek Concordance'. From simply knowing English, you can have access to have all the Greek words however they are translated into English. I know that a little knowledge is dangerous, and that we might leap to some unjustified conclusions, but if you want to find out where the different bits are, they're quite easily found.

Announcing the Messiah

Just a few more. Usually the word euangelion, as it is used, means to evangelise, not people, but you evangelise a message to people. That's the way it's usually used in the New Testament. So you are goodnewsing a message to the people. Now that's not universal, but it's the basic thing. So you find, for example, Luke 4:43, where Jesus says, 'it is binding upon me to evangelise the kingdom of God to all the cities.' Would that the church had taken that seriously!

The content of Jesus' evangel was the kingdom of God. Now once you understand it, the kingdom of God is Jesus Himself. Further on, in Paul, you find the phrase the kingdom of God used less and less because he's talking to Greeks who wouldn't understand that. So the content of the gospel becomes the Messiah, the Christ, the Jesus who is Lord. But, in fact, you're actually just looking at the beauty of the diamond from a different perspective when you say that the good news is the kingdom and the good news is Christ.

For Jesus, he was heralding and evangelising the kingdom of God (Luke 8:1). Again and again we get this word euangelion caught up with other words, which shows that Jesus wasn't divorcing it. We get an example in Luke 9:6 - evangelising and healing everywhere; Luke 16:16 - the kingdom of God is being evangelised and everyone is pressing towards it; Luke 20:1 - Jesus teaching the people and evangelising in the temple (and we have temples all around us today that have no knowledge of the gospel).

In Acts 5:42 we read that 'they didn't stop teaching and evangelising Jesus as the messiah.' The content of the evangelising is Jesus. They evangelised Jesus, and they evangelised Jesus as the Messiah, not as the super psychiatrist, as some of us have a tendency to do, but as the Messiah. That certainly means that Jesus brought healing and wholeness, but it's not the Jesus who deals with me privately and in isolation and who does the things I want. Jesus the Messiah knows where my health lies and has brought together a Messianic people and deals with us in the context of the Messianic people. In the relationships and love and healing between the people, He enables the people to be as free as He means them to be.

So our message must not be Jesus, but Jesus the Messiah.

Paul says, 'I have decided to know nothing among you, but Jesus the Messiah and Him crucified.' When I hear that text preached on, I hear people talking about the crucifixion, but that is not the message. Paul's message was the Messiah crucified and that makes a difference. Jesus was the Messiah and we rob it of its meaning if we make Christ or Messiah into a surname.

In Acts 8:4, euangelion appears in 'evangelising the word'. So here the content becomes the word. And in Acts 8:12, we've got Philip 'evangelising the things concerning the kingdom of God and the things concerning the name of Jesus the Messiah.' In 8:35, sharing with the Ethiopian, Philip evangelised Jesus to him.

And then 10:36, 'God is evangelising shalom through Jesus the Messiah, He is Lord of all,' so that shalom, the completeness that is God's gift, was the content of the good news. And that is the whole content of the kingdom of God all the way through the prophets: 'evangelising shalom through Jesus the Messiah, He is Lord.' 11:20 - 'evangelising the Lord Jesus.'

In 13:32, 'evangelising the promise made to the fathers.' Another way of looking at the good news is the promise made to the fathers. 15:35, 'evangelising the word of the Lord.' And right in the heart of the academics of his time, Paul speaking to the Epicureans and the Stoics was (17:18) 'evangelising Jesus and the resurrection' to them. I'll stop at that one.

In Luke the central thing was Jesus the Messiah. He was the gospel and fulfilled the promise made in the past, the very word of God. We experience Him in Jesus the Messiah, the Lord, who has died and has risen. I wonder if the good news that we have carries the full content of the kingdom with it?

Grace, gifts and joy
So, the messenger to the shepherds started off with sharing good news, 'Great joy to all people.' I'm not going to say a great deal about the word joy. It's a word that occurs 8 times in the gospel and 5 times in Acts. It's the word chara, joy. I'll read them for you, just to show where joy figures in Luke: 'thou shalt have joy and gladness'; 'bring you good tidings of great joy'; 'they received the word with joy'; 'the seventy returned again with joy'; 'likewise joy shall be in heaven'; 'there is joy in the presence of the Father'; 'though they yet believed not for joy' - that Jesus had risen. A strange one. It seems that their very joy at His presence actually interfered with their accepting the fact that He had risen.

In Acts we have: 'great joy in that city'; 'the disciples were filled with joy'; 'they opened up the gate for gladness' and Paul's final thing, 'that I might finish my course with joy.'

A quick thought and you're dependent on Greek for this bit. A student from London University asked me about grace and I gave him a definition. Then I thought, I'm a bit like a parrot here. So I said, 'Just a minute, I've got this new dictionary that's just come out, let's look it up there.' The book was a theological dictionary of the New Testament by Colin Brian and it really opened up a whole world to me. Brian said that chara, the word for joy, was part of the char group, which means well-being and charis, which we translate as grace, means that attitude within the heart of one person that moves towards the well-being of another. Chara is what that person experiences on receiving the well-being that comes from charis. So chara is what you receive, the joy is your response that comes up in you as the recipient of the charis or the grace of another.

Now this takes us to another word, a word that you at Post Green, under God, have a right to be with happy with. It's the word charisma, which is a very common New Testament word and it means an expression of charis. Charis is the word we usually translate as grace and it means the attitude in one person which moves towards the well-being of another. Call it kindness, call it love, call it concern, call it care, but I think it's more. I think it's the welling up in one person towards the well-being of another, that is charis. Chara is our experience of well-being from another. Joy is as close as we're going to get to it in English, but the words in English don't allow us to see the link up between the two. We experience joy as the response that comes as we receive the well-being from God's grace. Charisma is that which enables well-being, the gifts that God gives. Somebody calls them the grace gifts, that's pretty literal, but a good enough translation. Charisma is a grace gift; 'ma' at the end of the word suggests a gift or an expression, a token of.

An expression of God's love to us is charisma and the whole charismatic dimension of the body of Jesus is that dimension of our life whereby we live and we grow through the gifts of grace that God has distributed within the group. That's the primary understanding of charismatic and there's no way to get away from the fact that the New Testament community was a charismatic community. A community which existed and grew and developed as they shared and were open to the sharing of the grace gifts that God had given for their well-being and for the well-being of those outside the group. The charismatic gifts were not given

just so that we could become more complete, they were given so
that we could fulfil the mission that God has given us in the
world.

Eucharistia, of course, is another one. The eu at the beginning
is the same as the beginning of evangel, eu angelon. Eucharistia,
from which we get the word for thanksgiving is a different expression
of our response in personal terms for the well-being we've received.
Charis appears 9 times in the gospel and 16 times in Acts. Charis
was something that Luke was very aware of.

The People
Just a real quickie on the word for people as in 'great joy which
shall be to all people.' Paul uses this word 11 times, Matthew
15, Mark 3. Wait for it... Luke in his gospel, uses it 36 times
and in the Acts 49 times! Why was it that Luke was obsessed
with the concept of peoplehood?

He understood that God was about the creating of a people
- we emphasise individuality apart from peoplehood only by distorting
the message of the New Testament. The individuality that we must
affirm, that's central to the New Testament, is the individuality
which comes from peoplehood.

If you think of the individual cell of a honeycomb: it is single,
it is individual and unique, but if you try to remove the cell from
the honeycomb, you destroy something of six others because the
uniqueness of a cell in a honeycomb is given to it in relationships.
And God means us in His people to be unique, to be distinctive,
to be different one from the other, gloriously different. Every Christian
community that has tried to make everybody into sausages has
failed; every Christian community that has turned out people who
say the same things, look the same way, behave the same way,
practise the same way, has failed to be Christian community, because
God has made us distinctively different. Not in the individualistic
floating way, that allows us to wander in and out, but in the
way that we're related to one another in such a solidarity of life
that the one cell in the honeycomb having a cry makes the other
ones really damp; having a giggle and there's a shiver goes through
them all. That's just a different metaphor for what Paul calls the
Body of Christ.

However, we're like marbles, each one separate, each one complete
in itself. Take one out of a box of marbles and they might be
sorry to see it go, but nothing of them has gone. And that's how
the church is still functioning across the length and breadth of
Britain, as marbles in a collective with no understanding of joint

life and the corporate. One of the signs of hope that I see in Post Green is that you are working at an understanding of the corporate, the body, of sharing lives, of sharing possessions and actually doing the daring thing of giving somebody else the responsibility for your life, and of taking responsibility for theirs.

So the concept of the people is very, very important. This is the root of the word laity, the Greek word laos. The only trouble with that is that everybody was laity; they didn't have anybody who was a Christian who was not in the laos. It does not mean that within the laos there are not very different functions. Of course there are, but they are not the kind of functions that take you outside of the laos, to function as some kind of different being. Priesthood is a function of the whole laos, and nobody is made a priest in any sense that everyone is not made a priest, as far as the New Testament is concerned.

So, if someone is functioning as a priest, he is functioning representatively on our behalf, doing in that act what we are all doing in that act. Sometimes I wish that when we came in through our church doors we could all be given robes, so that we could understand that nature of priesthood. Apart from that, I'm not sure that they're not a hindrance to us today, because so many things are done by proxy and not representatively, and we're labelling and landing things on this poor guy up front - sadly, it is a guy - that sets us free from doing things.

That's another area where you're working very beautifully. There's an understanding of peoplehood that has released women in the way that Jesus did and has allowed men to grow from women. You haven't said to one part of the honeycomb, 'You're female, I have nothing to gain from you,' but have recognised that the way that God has put us together is very different from the way the old order was functioning, even among the Hebrew people.

Interestingly, liturgy is also based in all the people and shares the same root word. Liturgy is the word laos with the word ergon at the end of it, which means activity. So liturgy was actually an activity of all the people.

'...a saviour'

'Unto you is born this day a saviour.' I don't understand why, but that word saviour only appears twice in Luke's gospel and I don't think it appears in Acts at all. It first occurs in Luke 1:47, where Mary interestingly acknowledges that she needed a saviour. Mary says, 'my spirit has rejoiced in God my saviour' and I'm pleased about that. I love the character of Mary and there must be something very special about the woman that God chose to be the mother of His Son. God gave her the responsibility for the influences in Jesus' upbringing and life, influences which were such that Jesus stayed open to God.

I think some of us pull Mary down far too much and we don't realise the significant place she had, as the person at whose breast Jesus fed, on whose lap He learned all that He learned as a child, who taught Him the prayers He said, who taught Him the life of prayer. We really don't give the credit to Mary for who she was and what she did. But there may be others here for whom Mary has a different place and it's good to recall that, like ourselves, she recognised that God was her saviour.

This word salvation - Luke doesn't use the word saviour - the word salvation matters a great deal to him. I haven't even counted them up because I've got three pages of them. Salvation is a difficult word to grasp hold of in English. It's used in Luke, as in the whole of the New Testament, to cover a whole lot of different things.

Salvation was liberation from any situation that was unwhole into a situation that was whole for purposes of wholeness. Let me unpack that a wee bit. Salvation was salvation from something, it was salvation into something and it was salvation for something. It wasn't just salvation from, it was salvation for and to something. We weren't just saved from sin, we were saved from sin for something into something. It wasn't just sin that we were saved from. In fact, the word save is only connected with the word sin once and that's in Matthew 1.

The meaning of deliverance
Let's look at one or two of the things that salvation is deliverance from. For example, if we take the verb for the moment, it's the word that is used for health. When someone was got out of a situation of unwholeness, physical disease of one kind of another and was brought into a situation of wholeness, the word that was used there was salvation. It's even translated health.

We've got Jesus saying in Luke 8:47, 'your faith has saved you.' Other translations say, 'your faith has made you whole,' or, 'your faith has made you well,' because salvation is a making whole, a making well, a bringing out of unwholeness into wholeness. Luke 7:50, 'Your faith has saved you. Go into shalom.' The greeting was not 'Go in peace,' or 'Stop fighting,' or 'Have a sense of peace'; it was saying move on into wholeness. Jesus was saying, 'As a result of your trust, I have brought this measure of healing and wholeness to you, move on into shalom.' The only time that Jesus ever said 'Go in shalom' was when someone died. That's still true today.

So we've got Luke 8:36, where the man who was possessed with the demons was saved. He was liberated from something which was dominating and possessing his life, something to which he was captive. And if there is an area of our lives in which we are actually captive to something, then salvation is what we require. There are Christians who have unquestionably been saved because they are in Christ, who still need to be saved.

I became a Christian in the tradition where I was allowed to sit back and say, 'Ha, ha! I'm saved,' and I wasn't liberated. As I go round the country, I visit Christian Unions a lot. I can sit there with people who will triumphantly, sometimes arrogantly, shout, 'I'm saved!', but very often there is sadness in me when all I see are unliberated people, people who are not free, but anxious, uptight and screwed up. So, salvation is not just an event in God's purposes, though it is and we praise Him for that, it's an event which places us in the kingdom, but being in the kingdom in any area where we need liberation, we need salvation. That's salvation in terms of health.

It's also obviously the word that was used at the time when there was the shipwreck. For example, Acts 27:20 - 'all remaining hope that we might be saved was taken away.' Luke wasn't talking about a Salvation Army meeting, he was talking about being delivered from a situation of danger. They were actually about to lose their lives. Later, in 27:31, Paul says: 'if these men don't remain in the boat, you are not able to be saved.' So we've got to recognise that God's salvation extends to the preservation of our lives, to the bringing us out of situations of danger, to our being liberated from the fears and phobias that we've got. Salvation is all-encompassing.

Acts 14:9 takes us back to the healing usage of the word with the man who was crippled. Just before Paul says 'Stand up,' we find that the disabled man had faith to be saved, to be liberated from the thing that was crippling him.

It's used of political liberation as well. Acts 17:25 talks about how Moses thought his brothers knew that God was giving salvation through his hands. Now if you read that with the particular theological usage of salvation in mind, that becomes a difficulty. If we recognise that through Moses, God was bringing deliverance to people who were in captivity, we understand the nature of the salvation. Later on, in Timothy, Paul talks about women being saved in childbirth. That's also caused some problems to some people and might be

worth looking at. There's also the day of salvation that has come
to us, the salvation from enemies in Luke 1:71.

Jesus the liberator

An interesting case study of salvation is the story of Zacchaeus.
When Jesus speaks to Zacchaeus something happened to this little
twister, this little guy who sold himself out to the establishment
and was feathering his own nest, probably more from the poor
than from anybody else. Something happened as Jesus enters into
his whole stream of consciousness, his life, and he goes back and
he eats with Jesus in his home. Interestingly, Jesus took that initiative
and one of the things He says is, 'Today salvation has come to
this house.' That is, Zacchaeus has been liberated from greed, liberated
from selfishness.

We must be careful how we use that word salvation, so that
it covers the totality of those things which are not the way God
means them to be. At any place where life is not what God intended,
salvation is God's response. So when we talk about Jesus as the
saviour of the world, we're talking about Jesus as the liberator
par excellence at every level of our individual, corporate, societal,
global and universal being. Jesus is the liberator and the focal
point at which we see that the place of liberation in God's purposes
is the cross. Any understanding of Jesus as saviour which does
not move out and out and out and in and in and in, till we're
covering the totality of our lives is not doing justice to the nature
of His saviourhood.

To talk about Jesus as saviour and Jesus as Lord as if they
were two different things is a nonsense. It is the Lord who liberates;
He is the liberating Lord. People who say: 'I knew Jesus as my
saviour and then I came to know Him as my Lord' are going
through some experience. It may be very interesting, but it's not
a New Testament one, because the only Jesus we can know is
the Jesus who is Lord. And the only Lord we can know is the
Lord in His liberating of us and our knowledge of His Lordship
is in His liberating. So we have 16:17 of Acts, 'these persons
are slaves of the highest God, they are heralding the way of salvation.'

Eternal life

Let's take this a wee bit further and look at Luke 6:9, where
Jesus is talking about whether it's better to save a life or to kill
it. Life, here, is the Greek word psuche, which usually is translated
soul, as in the Authorised Version. The same word is used in
'whoever will save his own soul will lose it, whoever will lose

his own soul for my sake, will find it.'

The word psuche, soul, however, doesn't have the Greek philosophical meaning of something that indwells us, but refers to our total being which requires spirit to be alive. Without spirit, psuche is dead. It also requires body; as human beings, there is no living psuche without body. The New Testament doctrine is that death, which is the withdrawal of spirit, the withdrawal of lifebreath, means the end of me unless I am again given spirit and again given body.

Now the Greek philosophers believed that my body is insignificant, because the real me can continue without body. However, the New Testament is quite clear, and certainly the Old Testament is unequivocally clear, that the message of hope is the resurrection. I have no hope because I am immortal. My hope is in the grace of God, by which I will receive immortality as a gift of God in Jesus. Immortality is not inherent in me, it is a gift which has been brought to light by the gospel. God only has immortality and Christians who hold on to this vague philosophical and quite unbiblical idea that they are as inherently immortal as God is, are not thinking biblically and therefore the centrality and significance of the resurrection is dissipated.

Our hope is that God will bring us into a new existence with bodies that are different bodies, because they are not bodies of flesh with the limitations that we know. Apart from the body I am not me and apart from the spirit giving me life I am not alive. So we've got the New Testament metaphor of being asleep in Jesus until He comes. Some of you may not agree with that one, but the saving of the being and the losing of the being is quite an important one that comes in the gospels as well as later on.

A messiahed people

Quickly on to christos as in 'Jesus Christ, Christ the Lord'. It's almost only Luke who uses the verb that we actually use, the verb from which the name Jesus comes, the verb chriein. There's one in 2 Corinthians and one in Hebrews, but it is Luke's word. He is very conscious of the anointing of the Holy Spirit and the word anointing has two quite different words in the Greek.

One of them comes in James, where he talks about the anointing with oil. That's the word aleiphein and strictly that means to smear or to spread over or to cover. It was the anointing that happened to an athlete. If you were the kind of guy who had a slave who gave you a bath, he scraped you down and he anointed you, he gave you a massage and you felt great and your whole body felt tingling. It's like the kind of thing that happens among you, although you wouldn't call it anointing; when I see you going around affirming each other it is pretty close to what they mean. It was medical and it was athletic, but that doesn't mean it isn't theological. It means we get a warm glow from a massage or from someone who is of God.

This other word chriein is the kind of anointing that happened only at ordination. There were three groups of people in the Old Testament who were chrieined: the prophets, the priests and the kings. The Hebrew word for it is messiah. So if we coin a verb in English to be messiahed, there were three groups of people who were messiahed until the Messiah came. The Messiah, the anointed one, would come and he would be the prophet, the priest, the king, and then he would catch up into him those who trusted him and they would become the priests, the prophets, the kings in a priestly community, a prophetic community and a royal community.

So that messiahing or anointing is an ordination for service in the world. Messiahing is what God did to His Son, by which He fulfilled God's purposes among humanity, and as we trust in Christ we become messiah people. A Christian is a chriein and a real Christian is a person who has entered into the Messiah and who is in Christ. That means we have been anointed by the Spirit of God. I know this is central to a lot of your thinking, though you might not have used that word.

Luke 4:18, for example, is where Jesus stands up in the synagogue and says, 'The Spirit of the Lord is upon me.' Jesus did nothing as Messiah apart from the Spirit of God and the people who try to drive a wedge between Jesus and the Spirit are being utterly, utterly phoney. There is no way whereby we can be true to the Spirit of God without being centred on the Messiah. There is no way we can be people of the Messiah without recognising that he was the Messiah by the Spirit of God: 'The Spirit of God is upon me because He has messiahed me to evangelise the poor.' Acts 4:27, 'Jesus whom you have messiahed.' Acts 10:38, 'God messiahed Jesus of Nazareth in the Holy Spirit and in power. He went about doing good.' And that's the logical consequence of being a messiah people and yet there are many of us who know we're a messiah people to the extent that we're going about doing good.

The nature of the Messiah
Of the Messiah himself, Luke uses the word christos 13 times

in his gospel and 31 times in Acts. It's important to recognise that Jesus was recognised and acknowledged Himself to be the Messiah. There was clearly a lot of misunderstanding around what the Messiah was going to be like. And some of the sayings of Jesus about people keeping quiet about things seem to suggest that He did not want people to zone in on these misunderstandings about the nature of His messiahship or the kind of Messiah that He was, the person who came as the suffering servant and the son of man. Jesus took up particular understandings of Himself that the prophets had given, whereby He was certainly the son of man, but coming not in triumph, but to suffer as the servant for the people, and that was the nature of messiahship.

Perhaps it ought also to be seen as the nature of the messiahship of His people and that we are to participate in the fellowship of His suffering. We may have to be preparing ourselves openly before God, so that when we find ourselves suffering because we are working to turn the world upside down, we'll count it all joy because the suffering which we have entered in the Messiah.

So we've got Simeon looking at the baby Jesus, not knowing of the cross, not seeing the resurrected Christ, looking just at the baby and rejoicing that he had seen the Lord's Messiah. We've got people sending to John to see whether he was the Messiah in Luke 3:15.

Then we've got the demons; Luke's not at all prepared to hedge the realities that we find difficult. He's got the demons recognising that Jesus had power. I don't quite understand it, but the demons clearly recognise Him and Jesus silences them. 'You are the Messiah, the Son of God,' Luke 4:31. They knew that He was the Messiah. Even if we are hit with the realities that are hidden from us and kid ourselves, the demons are perfectly clear what's going on. In Paul's words, 'we wrestle not against flesh and blood but against principalities and powers.' We don't choose to be in a war, we are in it and if we're sitting in trenches and having our sandwich snack that goes on and on, that's no problem to the demonic. If we feel we've been given a lull, the war is on and we're complicit, either as a messianic people or we're furthering the purposes of the demonic.

'...the Lord'

Kurios, this word comes in Luke's gospel 104 times and in Acts 114 times, and that suggests that of all the things we've looked at, the way Luke sees Jesus was as Lord. Basically, this was a word that was in common usage for the person who had the right to command another. And we ought to recognise the first century as not really having a middle class at all - much more like parts of Africa and Asia, with a large differential between the people who had nothing and the people who had all the power. The people who had were always addressed as kurios by the people who had nothing, like the British 'sir', out of a kind of respect for somebody they believe to have significant superiority over them.

So when the woman of Samaria says 'sir', she uses kurios. But it's unlikely that she meant by that the full sense that the early church came to give it when they used that word of Jesus.

But over and above that everyday usage, in Acts 25:25 we've got Festus referring to the Roman emperor as the kurios. Here was the crucial one because when the Emperor started to be regarded as the kurios, the Christians were required to stand and say 'Caesar is kurios' and to join in every time that shout was used, and they wouldn't. And it was for that, for the recognition that the only person to whom they would given supreme loyalty was Jesus, that they were sent to the lions, they were tarred and stuck up on poles to light the garden parties that went on even in those days, because of their refusal to give that supreme authority to the state.

I suggest that we do just that. We're asked daily to give our supreme authority to someone other than Jesus and we've done it. Right now we in this room probably have areas of our lives where we are thoroughly polytheistic. We're not monotheistic at all, we just call them by a different name. The people who put their confidence in violence, who say they believe that Britain had just cause to go to war would find themselves the first to put their trust in violence. And how many Christians have we got who go along with that and the god of success, the Syrian god, Mammon? I know you're trying to disassociate yourselves from that here, but sometimes when you're doing that, it becomes even more important because you're giving an awful lot of attention to us. It's very difficult for us to give single-minded allegiance to Jesus in every area of our lives, except where we are open to the Spirit of God.

When the Alexandrian Jews were in exile in North Africa, they became very suave and sophisticated; they had to speak Greek, so they had to have their Bible in Greek. They had all these scrolls in Hebrew, but the people were so thoroughly urbane, urbanised and Hellenistic that they needed the Bible in Greek. So around 270BC the Hebrew Bible was translated into Greek.

I believe that was in God's purposes because if that hadn't

happened we wouldn't have a whole lot of what happened in the
New Testament, because the New Testament church basically used
that translation of the Old Testament. The fascinating thing is
that the Greek word they used for Yahweh, the sacred name of
God, was kurios. And again and again in the quotations of the
New Testament which refer to Jesus these are quotations from the
Old Testament which refer to Yahweh. So the early Christian
community, although they came from monotheistic Judaism,
unequivocally identified Jesus with Almighty God. I think sometimes
we forget that, that the one who we have experienced in tenderness
and love is God Himself among us. Utterly human, frail, wailing
as a kid, needing milk, needing attention, needing nurture: the
Almighty God.

The Messianic Jubilee

Introduction
It's nice to be back again. I know a whole lot of things have
happened since I was last here. I've heard about some of them,
Jeanne's told me a little bit on the way down in the car.

I thought that tonight we would turn to a specific passage and
try to consider on what basis the presentation of the ministry of
Jesus can be understood through the Jubilee. Now if it makes no
sense to you whatsoever, then that's fine for me because I'll be
breaking new ground. If you know it well, we'll get a chance
to share.

We'll take it from Luke 4, from verse 16, in the Good News
version. I'm going to concentrate particularly on that part of it
which gives some kind of light upon the whole basis from which
Luke sees the ministry of Jesus. (reads Luke 4:16-30)

It's a beautiful and fascinating story that Luke tells very beautifully
and I think it's got a whole lot of things for us. Some things
came not very long ago to me and one of the exciting things
in trying to bring our lives under a word of God that's living,
is that different things come to each of us at different times, things
that we've never seen at some time, suddenly shout out so that
we can't understand how we've ever missed them and things drift
away and we need to get them afresh.

I read something that I'd written on this passage and thought,
have I really seen that before? I had, it had just been removed
from my consciousness and from my obedience.

We'll return to the beginning of it in a few minutes, but I
want to do the background of this particular story, because there's
one line in the passage from Isaiah that Jesus was reading from,
Isaiah 61, the first two verses, where Jesus does an interesting

thing. He actually inserts a couple of verses from an earlier chapter into the middle of His quotation. We're not quite clear whether Jesus simply says, 'Hear this, and then back a couple of verses and hear this,' but it's taken from two separate little bits, it's not a direct quote from Isaiah 61. Where Jesus uses the phrase 'to proclaim the acceptable year of the Lord', that's the part of Isaiah that until recently we have all ignored when we've read that passage and it may hold the key to something very significant. A number of scholars today understand Luke to be making that particular affirmation a really significant one in terms of the whole ministry of Jesus.

We know that Jesus entered His public ministry when He was about 30 years old and that's in the year either AD26 or 27. The reason for the discrepancy is that the monk, Dionysius, who was responsible for putting the calendar together in the fifth century, made an error of about 4 years, so Jesus was actually born about 4BC. One of the fascinating things that has come to light in recent years has to do with that particular year, because in the Jewish calendar that was the fiftieth year, which is a year of Jubilee. I'll explain that in a moment because it takes us back into the Old Testament.

'The sabbath year'

The acceptable year of the Lord that Isaiah refers to is a year that was known as the year of Jubilee. That was the fiftieth year after seven times seven. Seven is a number that God seems to have decided on. The seventh day of the week, seven times seven, and then the year that followed it.

I wonder if you've ever thought of why the seventh day was set aside, why it was made distinctive? In Exodus 23:12 and Deuteronomy 5:14, you might be fascinated to find that the seventh day was set aside to give rest to the slave and to the alien. It was a time in which those who were serving us were set free from that service. It was a time of recreation for the oppressed. There are other reasons for the seventh day but that's quite clearly affirmed as primary.

In the seventh year, as God laid it down, all the land was to lie fallow for a whole year, the people were not to reap, not to sow, not to be involved in the ordinary work which was the very basis of their livelihood and their existence. For a whole year! And the purpose of that was that the land might be available to the oppressed and to the poor (Leviticus 25:1-7 and Exodus 23 10-11).

In that same seventh year, anyone who up to that time had found it necessary to go into service to another in order to pay his debts or whatever and had entered by those means into the only thing the Old Testament understands by slavery, was to be set free. That means that the longest period that a man could serve as a slave, being not self-sufficient but subservient to another, was seven years. (It might be interesting if we looked at our society and tried to understand what slavery is about today.) On that Old Testament basis, every seventh year the men who had had to sell themselves into the service of another were liberated and not only were they set free, but those to whom they were in bondage or service were required to give them the means that would allow them in their new freedom to avoid being slaves again. In other words, they didn't go empty handed. They were to be given the means of subsistence and the means of starting out afresh. References for that are Exodus 21:2 and Deuteronomy 15:12-18.

In that same year, the seventh, the sabbath year, all debts were to be cancelled. That meant clearly that if you were going to be a rotten type you incurred a debt when the seventh year was coming up, because come the seventh year it was scrubbed. Or if you were a rotten type on the other side with lots of money, you didn't allow to somebody to get one over you by lending or whatever, because you wouldn't get it back.

And again and again we find the prophets having to call people from this kind of selfishness, the selfishness which recognised what was coming up at the seventh year and put the economy in trouble because the wealthy held on to their money rather than put it at risk and others took loans with no thought of paying them back. This was among God's people! But God's purpose, and it's spelled out clearly in Deuteronomy 15:1-11, was that debts were to be cancelled and on the day of Jubilee every person within the people of God was a free man, free of debt to any other man and free of debt to God.

The Jubilee year

Now seven times seven gives you forty-nine and the forty-ninth year was a sabbath year, and the year following the sabbath year was the year of Jubilee. So in the year of Jubilee the land lay fallow for two years. And that was actually not just doing something valuable for the soil, because before they had our way of doing things, that was rather important, but it was also putting an enormous test on the people's faith, that God would actually provide for them if they didn't plough, didn't sow and didn't reap for two solid years.

But one thing that was distinctive about the Jubilee year, that caused a great deal of problems, was that the land was redistributed. Every fiftieth year whoever had lost land from their clan or from their family, the land that had been given them by God, lost it either by mismanagement, getting into debt, or by death or any of the other means by which the wealth and poverty of people is determined - they were given back their land. Every fiftieth year there was a redistribution of land back to how it was when God distributed it, so that none of the families went without land. Now we find very little evidence in the Old Testament that this was ever carried out. I don't know if we can place a lot of emphasis on the silence, some scholars try to, but clearly this was a major thing (Leviticus 25:8).

One or two things before we take this further, and into the New Testament. The Jubilee year was a holy year. We're accustomed today to holy days which we've turned into a word which does not even sound as if it's meant to be distinctive, although to some of us it is - holiday. But they had a holy year - the fiftieth year was distinctive to God and set apart specifically for the oppressed and the poor, for those who couldn't manage, for the little people, the folk who couldn't cope, for the inadequate, for those who'd fallen into debt.

Every one returned to his or her own family (Leviticus 25:10;13) for the beginning of the Jubilee year to his own family. They went back to their own village, back to their own community. It began on the day of Atonement (Leviticus 25:9). In other words, it began with the festival among Hebrew people at which an animal was sacrificed, the only time in the year, and the high priest entered the Holy of Holies in the temple. And the people entered as a people into a renewal of their covenant relationship with God because their sins were carried by that animal which representatively, and in their phrase, 'carried their sin before God'.

God's promise was to supply the one of whom that animal was a symbol, that is 'the suffering servant' who was to come. The suffering servant was strongly emphasised in Isaiah and strong in the passage that Jesus reads: the suffering servant who was to come 'and the chastisement of our shalom was to be upon him and by his stripes we were to be healed.' So the day of Atonement was looking forward to the time when the very servant of God would die as a representative in the place of the people and be the means of reconciling the people to God.

It also looked to the beginning of the very nature of the kingdom of God and the community of God's new covenant. Now it's fascinating that the Jubilee year began when the people themselves were in a new relationship with God. It began when in the temple that act, which was the symbolic act of God's love and God's reconciliation, had taken place and the people were set free before God and placed in a new relationship with one another before Him. Because of what had happened in the day of Atonement, and as a direct response to that, they went out into a situation where everyone was free in relation to everyone else, where debts were scrubbed, where prisons were emptied (such as the prisons were), and where new relationships were created and the land redistributed.

There was a whole context of joy as the people who had been the failures were able to stand up straight again and as the people who had benefitted from their failure had bowed before God and been forgiven. And oppressor and oppressed, both were in a new relationship with God and a new relationship with one another and found a new dignity within themselves.

So this vision of the Jubilee year is a very, very exciting one to which the prophets turn again and again. We're given several places in the Old Testament where it's actually mentioned; Numbers 36, Ruth 3-4 and Jeremiah 34, if you want to chase it up.

Fulfilling the Jubilee

The Jubilee year started with a trumpet. Jubilee comes from the word jubil, by the way, which was the ram's horn which was sounded by the priests, and the only one who had the right to take up that trumpet and blow it was the priest, which means that Jesus standing up in the synagogue was actually taking upon himself the sounding of the trumpet. He was making not just one claim.

Now if we go back to Luke and ponder some of his words. I think I've covered most of what I wanted to say from the Old Testament. We've looked at the blowing of the horn, liberty for the lamb, Leviticus 25:10, ownership of land restored to where it was when Joshua parcelled it out at the time of the conquest and the reason for the original royal grant of land: 'the land is mine and you are strangers and sojourners in it.' So there's a very different understanding of the ownership of land. It's not public ownership, it's not private ownership, it's God ownership. And just as nobody today in Britain would dream of laying claim to the air, (they do lay claim to the water, and to the seaside), the Hebrews were quite clear that the land was God's and that at best they occupied it as tenants.

We've looked at the economic implications: when the land was bought or sold, the transaction was valid only until the year of Jubilee when it reverted to the original owner. No land could be sold in perpetuity and the value of land was determined by the number of years remaining until the Jubilee. The more the years, the greater the price. But ultimately it meant that nobody really bought the land; all you bought was a number of harvests, and a pretty limited number at that.

But of greater importance than the price of the land was the effect that it had upon the entire social system. The effect upon wealth and poverty was great, as it meant that had the people stood by God's provision of the year of Jubilee, there would have been no permanently poor people, no permanently wealthy people and no super rich, because it was a leveller that restored people to the dignity that God had meant them to have.

Now this is taken up again and again in references in the prophets to the kingdom of God. And there are some who think that rather than looking to the Jubilee, or the kingdom as a picture of the Jubilee, we should look to the Jubilee as a picture of the kingdom. In fact if Jesus was using the Jubilee year then, He was using it to illustrate the nature and the content of the kingdom of God.

Just a few things that are of interest that tie up with the Old Testament understanding of the Jubilee. It does seem likely that the year that Jesus entered his ministry was literally the year that should have been the year of Jubilee, AD26-27. The lectionary (though some scholars question whether the lectionary went right back as far as Jesus) that was in use for the sabbath day before the Atonement in the earliest records we've got for the synagogue, is Isaiah 61:10,11. We find that in Luke 4 Jesus returned to Nazareth where He had been brought up, which was required of people just before the Jubilee began. Further, we find that Jesus takes up the very text that was read before the Atonement. I would suggest that there's a lot to be said for seeing that Jesus Himself believed that in Himself the year of Jubilee was fulfilled and that He was introducing the kingdom of God, which among the people of God, was to be a permanent Jubilee.

This Jubilee meant that men and women who came in on the day of Atonement, through the blood of the lamb, to be brought right with God, were required in that moment to be right with one another, were required in that moment to set one another free from any debts, were required in that moment to set anyone free from subservience, were required to release those who were in prison, were required to bring good news to the poor, were required to bring recovery of sight to the blind. Now, if that's what Jesus is about, it has some very important and significant things to say to us.

'Physician, heal yourself.'

Jesus anticipated the response of the people when He took up the words 'Physician, doctor, heal yourself. Do the miracles among us that you've done in Capernaum, and we'll believe you.' You'll recall that just before this some significant things had happened, almost right at the beginning of Luke's gospel.

Last time we looked at the significance, for Luke, of the angelic annunciation of Jesus, as the one who was to be Messiah and Lord. Then Luke presents the baptism and the clear declaration that Jesus received and John heard. Then the driving by the Spirit into the wilderness where He was tempted for 40 days and 40 nights. There in the wilderness Jesus was being tested, I believe, about the nature of His messiahship, the kind of messiah He was to be: whether He would avoid the cross; whether He would avoid being the suffering servant that He clearly understood He must be; and whether He would bring together the understandings of the Old Testament prophets of the suffering servant and the son of man.

We can understand why so many of the Jewish people didn't accept Jesus as Messiah, because there were two quite different strands coming through the prophets, which no-one until Jesus had brought together. One was the son of man coming in clouds of glory to set up a kingdom, and this was the one that they had zoned in on as the Messiah. The other, which they had never thought of as referring to the Messiah, was the suffering servant who was going to come and was going to die for the people. They had no concept of a Messiah who was going to suffer. Jesus was the one who brought together the two ideas in one person: the son of man, who would come in glory, who was none other than the servant, who would come and who would suffer on behalf of the people.

This was one of the difficulties they had; even the disciples had trouble coming to terms with that. And after the resurrection, on the walk to Emmaus, Jesus had to say, 'Ought not the Messiah to suffer these things and to enter into his glory?' Right to the very end then, they were having difficulty in understanding the nature of the Messiah as the one who suffered.

But the response from the people of Nazareth in Luke 4 was

that they wanted to see a miracle: 'If this was the year of Jubilee, show us the miracles then.' When Jesus had come out of the wilderness and gone into Capernaum, He'd done some marvellous things and coming up to the day of Atonement, He'd gone in and made this Jubilee declaration. The people were excited but I find Jesus making this kind of response: 'It would be inappropriate. The Jubilee is not a grace from God that we sit back and receive. The Jubilee is an active response to the grace of God. The Jubilee year is involving us in trust, involving us in obedience, involving us in a whole new releasing of others into the people of God.

It's not a case of saying, "Physician, heal thyself"; it's not a case of seeing miracles. Miracles will come as part of God's response to our response to His initiative.' And I think that Jesus is saying: 'You're sitting there on your backsides asking me to do magic, to prove something to you that you're not really waiting to have proved at all. Jubilee is what God has asked, required of you, as His people. Jubilee is your response to the Atonement.'

Jesus goes on - and I used to think these next verses were an intrusion that interrupted the whole thing. I now see what He is saying. Israel has been disobedient again and again and again. They have refused to respond in Jubilee to God's initiative and God has, for that reason, turned aside from them and has worked among the Gentiles. And Jesus is saying more than that: 'Right now, while you sit there on your backsides, asking me for magic, sitting there in your disobedience, God is about to turn and the Jubilee is offered to the Gentiles.' He quite clearly points out to them what had happened in the day of Elijah and the day of Elisha. In both cases God turned, in the one case to a woman from Sidon and in the other to Naaman the Syrian, neither of them from among the chosen people of God.

Luke gets so excited every time Jesus turns His attention to the people who are not among the chosen people, because he wasn't one of the chosen people himself. And he gets very excited every time he hears Jesus saying something that really affirms inside him his experience of God's grace and God's love, so he tells us bits that the others don't tell us. Matthew is very fond of telling us 'the scripture is fulfilled'. It's different looking at it through the eyes of Matthew, who had been brought up among the people of God, from Luke, who knew the blessings had nothing to do with heritage, but something unique and very special.

And so the fact that Jesus said this quite clearly in a synagogue was what upset the congregation. They could take all the rest of it, were quite happy about it, but as soon as He mentioned that

God's grace and God's initiative had reached out to the Gentiles, that the kingdom of God was going to reach to the Gentiles and they were going to be incorporated into the people of God, they went mad. Jesus clearly had the sense of God's total presence, so He wasn't manipulated. If you look at the number of times in Luke's gospel that it says Jesus 'must' do such and such, it seems there was a kind of compulsion, that Jesus moved around with a sense of appropriateness. The openness that Jesus had to the Father meant that He knew the appropriateness of the right moment for this, that and the other.

'Good news to the poor'

The good news is the ordinary word for evangelism - euangelion. I would like sometimes to look at just how the word evangelism is used. It's a much wider thing than some of us have allowed it to be and I wonder whether evangelism to the poor or goodnewsing the poor, as it was used by Isaiah, means what we would mean today by goodnewsing the poor. I have my doubts.

The poor, we recognised, means the people who are doubled up, the kind of people who are in a dependent relationship to others, the kind of people who find they are doffing the cap to life because they can't stand up straight and have no sense of personal worth. Their whole worth comes out of their dependency upon others. That's not how God wants His people to be, that's not how He made us to be.

There is a right kind of humility that we enter as we look one another in the eye and choose to be subservient one to the other. That's a quite different thing from having people who are trodden on, who don't choose to be anything. And the poor are those who have been reduced to the point where they cringe and they back away. And it's quite clear that Jesus had a very strong identity with the poor, and if we look in Isaiah 61, there's no way that we can turn that language into metaphorical language.

We glorify the metaphorical by the word 'spiritual' at times. It doesn't make sense to spiritualise things. If something is made spiritual, it is made open to the Holy Spirit and I can't handle any other meaning than that. If we mean by spiritualise that we turn it away from realism, then that's a denial of the Holy Spirit; it's wrong to say that to spiritualise means to make something unrealistic. If we turn this into a metaphor then we are denying that Jesus is talking about people who are poor.

Every one of us here is wealthy. There's not one of us going without food, not one of us without friends, not one of us who hasn't got the personal freedom to understand life and to read the signs of the times or where we are in relationships. Not one of us. So to call ourselves poor is a nonsense. Jesus is not talking about us, He's talking about people to whom we have a responsibility. I know there are other ways of being poor, but I think we avoid the judgement of \God and we avoid the call to the participation in Jubilee if we don't recognise the poor and the underprivileged and the dispossessed in the world.

It's a tragedy that even the people caught up in the movement of the Spirit think that it is a personal luxury that they enjoy, but it doesn't drive them out to a place of need. I find it very hard to think that we can be in obedience to the Spirit when we are not in solidarity with the people with whom Jesus was.

'...to proclaim freedom'

To proclaim, that's the word for a herald, and I find that fascinating. The interesting thing about the message as it comes through a herald - and I wish it wasn't translated preach. I really think the demonic got into the translators when they say preach, because we always think it's somebody else, never us. We've all been made a herald in community.

The distinctiveness about the herald was that he was handed the message he had to announce by the local governor or the king. He wasn't free to stand up and say, 'Well, I was told to say this, but I prefer to say this,' or 'I'll miss this little bit out because such and such.' The thing about a herald is that he was given a set message, which he was not free to alter and which he declared with boldness, because he was not responsible for it.

And if there's one dimension that we as God's people need right now, it's an awareness of what it means to be God's heralds. There are loads and loads of people who are happy to say, 'Well, it could be this and it could be that.' There are very few who are prepared to stand up and be heralds. And to have a community whose life is at one with its words would be, to me, something of what the New Testament is about.

I'm going to read a bit from Leviticus 25 and see if you recognise why I've taken this passage: 'If you say what shall we eat the seventh year, since we neither sow nor harvest, I will give you my blessing on the sixth year and it will produce enough.' Now look at Luke 12:29-31: 'Don't be anxious and don't say what shall we eat. Seek first the kingdom and justice of God and all these things shall be added to you.' If we put the words of Jesus into the context of His reflection on God's word and His understanding of it, we would come to a much surer grasp of what the message was about.

Even the Lord's Prayer is so completely interpenetrated with the language of Jubilee that it's almost a Jubilee prayer, and particularly in Luke. Luke and Matthew have different versions. In Scotland, interestingly enough, we use Luke's version, but down here you all seem to use Matthew. There are two different words: 'Forgive us...' - I now instinctively say 'trespasses', because that's the way you say it down here, but Luke has 'forgive us our debts as we forgive our debtors.' It actually means debts. Now that's quite fantastic, Jesus is tying up our indebtedness to God and our release from indebtedness to Him with our actual literal openness and release of others from any debt that they have to us.

I think that that message needs to be heard today. It is significant that in a world where the poor of the Third World are crying out to God for such a release from indebtedness and poverty, that we in the West continue to act as though we had no responsibility for causing the problems that they face. But that history of exploitation we don't find in the history books we read; it's in the history books being read in Africa and Asia and Latin America. We say, 'That's Marxist propaganda,' but I think some people are further removed and are able to say what motivated and who benefitted.

The church as an institution is going to be found not to have stood with the poor and the oppressed, but to have stood again and again with the wealthy and the oppressor. And I don't know how we bring ourselves as a community of God's people into solidarity with the poor when we are so entrenched ourselves as beneficiaries of the past.

'The Spirit of the Lord is upon me'

But I'm completely convinced of this little bit. Jesus begins what He says in the synagogue in verse 18: 'The Spirit of the Lord is upon me wherefore He anointed me.' Those of you who are studying the Greek with me will find that interesting. This is one of the places where translators have problems. There is no punctuation in Greek whatsoever and no gaps between words. And this is where we don't know where the full stop comes. Some of the translators, and it may be in some of your Bibles have, 'the Spirit of the Lord is upon me, wherefore, by which, He anointed me.' Full stop. 'He has sent me to bring good news to the poor, to proclaim release to the captives...' Most of the older versions have 'the Spirit of the Lord is upon me because, or wherefore, or by which means, He has anointed me to proclaim good news to the poor.'

I can't solve it for you. There is no resolution to it. We don't know. It could mean that the messiahship was to bring good news to the poor - 'He messiahed me to do this' and that's quite strong because it links the function of being messiah to the poor.

'The Spirit of the Lord' - the word used for Lord is kurios, the same as we mentioned before. What is interesting is that in the Old Testament the word kurios is reserved for God's name, for Yahweh and in the New Testament it is used of Jesus. And this is the most fascinating affirmation within the Jewish Christian community, that in a monotheistic community (and there's no question that Peter, James, John, and the rest of them were thorough monotheists) they used the word kurios for Jesus.

Of course, the word was used in other simple ways too. People who joined the Roman army had to stand up and give the salute and say 'Caesar is kurios.' And one of the reasons why Christians wouldn't take part in the war was because they wouldn't join the army and, if they were in it, they came out. Some people think the early church was totally pacifist because to be in the army was to stand up and say that Caesar was kurios, which they refused to do. If we were asked today who was Lord, it might be interesting.... In the early church it wouldn't be like that. All areas were under the Lordship of Jesus and I suspect the easy way to accommodate compromise is to give different people their lordships. We don't find the early church doing that.

'He has anointed me'

The Living Bible has 'He has chosen me.' The word there is echrisen; chris in the middle of it, the beginning of the word christos. It's the word to anoint. And the Hebrew for to anoint is messiah. So, if this verse was put into the Hebrew or the Aramaic in which it was probably heard, it would be, 'the Spirit of Yahweh is upon me, by which He has messiahed me.' Anointing in the Spirit is messiahing.

Luke later takes this up in Acts 10, where Peter speaks in response to Cornelius's request and Peter stands up and gives his statement, from verse 34. Some of you may love it, I know I do, Acts 10, verse 34. I think we might just about finish with this because it speaks about us. If we are the Messiah people, if we are anointed in the Spirit of God, messiahed in the Spirit of God. And all that Jesus did He did because He was messiahed in the Spirit. And all that He did He did in the power of the Spirit. The whole messianic work that Jesus took up in relation to the poor, to the blind and the oppressed and the crushed -

that last one I should have taken time on - the people who are crushed, the oppressed ones - all of that He did in the power of the Spirit.

And if we are to be a messianic people, the people in the Messiah - Paul talks about being in Christ and at Antioch they were called christianoi, that means messiah people - if we are to be messiah people, it will only be by the messiahing of the Holy Spirit. And I think sometimes when we talk about the action of the Holy Spirit in our lives we're thinking in very personal terms. And we should, because God deals with us as individual people, but the messiahing is also into the Messiah community, to be the Messiah people and to do things in our togetherness that are greater. He said, 'Greater things than these shall ye do,' and He has actually enabled the doing of greater things than He, as Messiah, did through His people as they are open to the Spirit. And I really believe that.